A
Summer
Greek
Reader

A
Summer Greek Reader

A WORKBOOK FOR MAINTAINING YOUR BIBLICAL GREEK

Richard GOODRICH
and
David DIEWERT

ZONDERVAN™

GRAND RAPIDS, MICHIGAN 49530 USA

ὑπὲρ τῶν μαθητῶν ὑμῶν

ZONDERVAN™

A Summer Greek Reader
Copyright © 2001 by David Diewert and Richard Goodrich

Requests for information should be addressed to:

Zondervan, *Grand Rapids, Michigan 49530*

ISBN: 0-310-23660-6

The Greek text used for this book is the Greek text on which the NIV translation was based, as developed by John R. Kohlenberger III. Used by permission of John R. Kohlenberger III. All rights reserved.

Interior design by Nancy Wilson

Printed in the United States of America

04 05 06 07 08 09 /❖ VG/ 10 9 8 7 6 5 4

Contents

Acknowledgments

We would like to thank Doris Evanson for her thoughtful critique of an early version of this book. A warm thanks also to our editor, Verlyn Verbrugge, whose sure hand guided this book through the shoals and reefs of the publishing process. Regent College's Introductory Greek Class (1998/1999) inspired this text, and from that class we would like to single out Erik Johnson and Eric Stelle for their tenacious field testing of this manuscript. Finally, we would like to thank our wives (Mary and Teresa) and families for the lost hours. Without their ungrudging sacrifice this book would not have become a reality. It is as much their book as ours.

Preface

Students who have just completed an introductory biblical Greek class are in an unenviable position. Over the course of a year, they have expended a prodigious amount of time and energy to master the morphology of Greek words, some simple grammar, and a rudimentary vocabulary. The students have translated simple sentences, committed convoluted paradigms to memory, and agonized over parsing exercises.

An incredible amount of work goes into a yearlong introductory Greek class, and it is natural that, at the end of it, students should want to enjoy some of the fruit of that sustained labor. They would like to begin reading the Greek New Testament, and it seems unfair that after such a dedicated effort the student is not able to open a Nestle-Aland or UBS text and begin reading.

Professors are often faced with students who ask for a recommendation for summer reading. The students would like (quite rightly) to continue practicing Greek over the summer. A little extra work maintains proficiency, which gives the students confidence when starting intermediate Greek. Moreover, reading Greek over the summer is a reward for the effort spent learning these skills.

Unfortunately, until now we have never had anything to offer the students who want to continue using their Greek over the summer. As William Mounce astutely notes in his *Graded Reader of Biblical Greek,* the biblical text contains "hard realities."[1] An introductory level student is not equipped to read most of the New Testament. Not only are there strange grammatical constructions in the text, but even the simpler verses are riddled with vocabulary words that occur fewer than fifty times. The students simply do not have the vocabulary base necessary to avoid frequent trips to the lexicon, and they quickly learn that a well-thumbed lexicon is a wearisome thing. More often than not, students who begin a course of summer reading simply abandon the effort after a few days and will not study Greek until the intermediate Greek class begins.

A Summer Greek Reader has been designed to address this situation. With a little help, students can work through a number of texts over a summer and return to intermediate Greek with a much better grasp of the language than the students who neglect it over a summer. Our summer reader is designed for students who have just completed introductory Greek and desire texts that are suitable for that level. We have selected our texts with the following four goals in mind:

1. To help students retain Greek skills over a summer. A Summer Greek Reader is designed for students who want to apply the skills learned in introductory Greek. Its main purpose is to maintain skills rather than to develop new ones. Consequently, this book does not attempt to teach grammar or syntax. Advanced skills will be further refined in the classroom during intermediate Greek.

2. To allow the students, working independently, to translate lengthy selections from the Greek New Testament. We have designed *A Summer Greek Reader* for use over a twelve-week period. Each week focuses on a single block of text, consisting of thirty to thirty-five verses. This block is

---

[1]William Mounce, *A Graded Reader of Biblical Greek* (Grand Rapids: Zondervan, 1996), viii.

divided into six daily readings of four to seven verses. Each daily selection should take no more than fifteen to twenty minutes to translate. Students may choose to work through a selection every morning as part of their devotional time.

There is much to be said for working with longer selections of text. Individual verses, though useful for didactic illustration, are somewhat artificial. Students who work with longer selections begin to gain an appreciation for the role of context in translation. Moreover, they will be one step closer to the ultimate goal of biblical Greek classes—working with the Greek text.

To facilitate independent use, a rough translation of each selection is provided in the back of this workbook. These translations follow the Greek text more literally than modern English translations do. They are not in good, idiomatic English, but rather have been done in a way that accurately reflects the Greek in these verses. This allows the students to check their work more easily, eliminating the "How did they get that translation?" factor.

3. To allow the student to continue building a vocabulary of New Testament Greek. Although Mounce's series of biblical Greek books is by far the best and most usable series available today, it does suffer from one small deficiency. The *Basics of Biblical Greek* textbook teaches vocabulary that occurs in the Greek New Testament fifty times or more. Mounce's second-year graded reader, *A Graded Reader of Biblical Greek,* defines words in

footnotes that occur twenty or fewer times in the Greek New Testament. Those words occurring twenty-one to forty-nine times have fallen through the crack. Consequently, students beginning an intermediate Greek class that uses *A Graded Reader* find that they have a lot of vocabulary to learn in a hurry.

A Summer Greek Reader introduces that vocabulary in this period between introductory and intermediate Greek, rather than having students try to cram it in during the first weeks of the new school year. It divides these missing words over eleven chapters.[2] As the students work through the book, they memorize the new vocabulary and read selections that focus on these new words. The students learn the new words and then use them in translations.

4. To help students enjoy reading the Greek New Testament. In order to accomplish this, all unfamiliar words are cross-referenced or defined in footnotes. Consequently, students may use this reader without having to thumb through a lexicon. This greatly enhances the speed and joy of reading.

We hope this text will develop a deep and abiding love for the Greek New Testament in its readers. Used diligently, *A Summer Greek Reader* will ease the transition between introductory and intermediate Greek. We hope our small contribution to the world of Greek scholarship will place our readers in a better position as they begin the challenging work of intermediate Greek.

Richard Goodrich
David Diewert
Regent College, 1999

---

[2]The first chapter of *A Summer Greek Reader* uses the vocabulary given in Mounce's *Basics of Biblical Greek.* The following chapters introduce twenty to thirty new vocabulary words each week.

Using *A Summer Greek Reader*

Congratulations on your desire to pursue further Greek reading. Used diligently, *A Summer Greek Reader* will allow you to maintain the translation skills you have acquired in introductory Greek.

A Summer Greek Reader is divided into twelve chapters. Ideally, you will work through one chapter a week, translating the passage and memorizing the new vocabulary. Each chapter is divided into three sections: six passages[1] for you to translate, an English translation to check your work, and a list of new vocabulary for you to learn.

Translation Passages

The translation passages featured in *A Summer Greek Reader* have been selected with two criteria in mind: familiar vocabulary and straightforward syntax. Our goal is to provide you with passages you can read rather than with knotty tangles to unravel.

Unfamiliar vocabulary is defined in footnotes and/or cross-referenced elsewhere in this reader. Definitions consist of lexical form, English definition, and the number of occurrences of the word in the Greek New Testament. For instance, look at Reading 4 of Week One (footnotes 13 and 14):

> [13]πώποτε, *ever, at any time* (6).
> [14]θεάομαι, *I see, look at* [Vocab. 11].

The "(6)" after πώποτε indicates that πώποτε occurs six times in the Greek New Testament. The "[Vocab. 11]" entry after θεάομαι indicates that the word may be found in the vocabulary list for chapter 11. Unfamiliar vocabulary is defined once each page. If a word was defined earlier in a chapter, a reference to the first occurrence of the word will be provided. For example, see footnote 18 of Reading 5 of Week One:

> [18]See verse 12.

If you stumble across a word you do not recognize, first check the footnotes in the section you are translating.

Each selection also features underlined words for parsing practice. You will find the full parsing for the underlined words with the English translations. Not only does this allow you to continue practicing your parsing, but it also allows you to look up some of the more difficult forms if you cannot parse them.

English Translations

The English translations are provided so that you can check your work. They are not the best translations of the passages. They are raw and unpolished. You would not want to quote them in a sermon. Nevertheless, they do follow the Greek text with a clumsy literalism. At this stage of your learning, you will find them more helpful for understanding the Greek text than a modern English translation like the NIV.

Words that do not appear in the Greek text but seem necessary to smooth out the sentence are inserted in square brackets. For example, see 1 John 4:14 in Reading 4 of Week One: "And we have seen and we bear witness that the Father has sent the Son, [as] Savior of the world."

Note one other thing: The writers of the narrative portions of the Greek New Testament frequently switch between the aorist tense and

---

[1]One for each day of the week, not counting Sunday.

the present tense (this latter use is called the historical present). In the translations, it seems best to keep the sort of consistency we are used to in English (either all past tense or all present tense); thus, many present tense verbs will be translated as a past tense.

Vocabulary Lists

You will find a list of new vocabulary words at the end of each chapter (except chapter 1, which uses the vocabulary that occurs fifty times or more in the Greek New Testament). If you memorize these lists as you work through *A Summer Greek Reader,* you will know all of the words that occur in the Greek New Testament twenty or more times. This will help you immensely in intermediate Greek. It will also enhance your enjoyment of other parts of the Greek New Testament. We have found that enjoyment is inversely proportional to the number of words you have to look up in a lexicon.

In an attempt to help you learn new vocabulary, we have divided the new words into three categories: *Friends, Cousins,* and *Strangers. Friends* are words that bear a strong resemblance either to a Greek word you have already learned or to an English word. *Cousins* are those words that have a more distant resemblance to familiar Greek or English words; if you squint when you look at them, you will see a family likeness. *Strangers* are words that we could not readily tie to a Greek word you knew or to a familiar English word. When possible, we have offered quirky and whimsical memory aids for the strangers, believing that memorization is facilitated if the brain has something unusual to link to a word.

Look over the vocabulary list before beginning a new chapter of *A Summer Greek Reader.* Words that occur in the chapter's vocabulary list (as well as in the vocabulary lists of preceding chapters) will not be defined in the footnotes for a passage.

We have consulted the word frequency lists in *The Student's Complete Vocabulary Guide to the Greek New Testament* by Warren Trenchard (Grand Rapids: Zondervan, 1992) in designing these sections. We strongly recommend this book for students who want to broaden their Greek vocabulary base.

Abbreviations

BAGD   *A Greek-English Lexicon of the New Testament and Other Early Christian Literature.* W. Bauer. Translated and revised by W. F. Arndt, F. W. Gingrich, and F. W. Danker. Chicago: University of Chicago Press, 1979.

BBG   *Basics of Biblical Greek.* William D. Mounce. Grand Rapids: Zondervan, 1993.

Wallace   *Greek Grammar Beyond the Basics.* Daniel B. Wallace. Grand Rapids: Zondervan, 1996.

Week One

1 John 3:22–5:6

Reading 1 | 1 John 3:22–24

22. καὶ ὃ ἐὰν <u>αἰτῶμεν</u> λαμβάνομεν ἀπ᾿ αὐτοῦ, ὅτι τὰς ἐντολὰς αὐτοῦ τηροῦμεν καὶ τὰ ἀρεστὰ[1] ἐνώπιον αὐτοῦ ποιοῦμεν. **23.** καὶ <u>αὕτη</u> ἐστὶν ἡ ἐντολὴ αὐτοῦ, ἵνα πιστεύσωμεν τῷ ὀνόματι τοῦ υἱοῦ αὐτοῦ Ἰησοῦ Χριστοῦ καὶ ἀγαπῶμεν ἀλλήλους, καθὼς ἔδωκεν ἐντολὴν ἡμῖν. **24.** καὶ ὁ <u>τηρῶν</u> τὰς ἐντολὰς αὐτοῦ ἐν αὐτῷ μένει καὶ αὐτὸς ἐν αὐτῷ· καὶ ἐν τούτῳ γινώσκομεν ὅτι μένει ἐν ἡμῖν, ἐκ τοῦ πνεύματος οὗ[2] ἡμῖν ἔδωκεν.

Parsing: αἰτῶμεν _____

αὕτη _____

τηρῶν _____

Translation:

_____

_____

_____

_____

_____

_____

_____

_____

_____

_____

_____

_____

_____

_____

_____

---

[1]ἀρεστός, -ή, -όν, *pleasing* (4).   [2]Can you explain the case of this word?

Reading 2 | 1 John 4:1–6

1. Ἀγαπητοί, μὴ παντὶ πνεύματι πιστεύετε, ἀλλὰ δοκιμάζετε[3] τὰ πνεύματα εἰ ἐκ τοῦ θεοῦ ἐστιν, ὅτι πολλοὶ ψευδοπροφῆται[4] <u>ἐξεληλύθασιν</u> εἰς τὸν κόσμον. **2.** ἐν τούτῳ γινώσκετε τὸ πνεῦμα τοῦ θεοῦ· πᾶν πνεῦμα ὃ ὁμολογεῖ Ἰησοῦν Χριστὸν ἐν σαρκὶ <u>ἐληλυθότα</u> ἐκ τοῦ θεοῦ ἐστιν, **3.** καὶ πᾶν πνεῦμα ὃ μὴ ὁμολογεῖ τὸν Ἰησοῦν ἐκ τοῦ θεοῦ οὐκ ἔστιν· καὶ τοῦτό ἐστιν τὸ τοῦ ἀντιχρίστου,[5] ὃ <u>ἀκηκόατε</u> ὅτι ἔρχεται, καὶ νῦν ἐν τῷ κόσμῳ ἐστὶν ἤδη.

4. ὑμεῖς ἐκ τοῦ θεοῦ ἐστε, τεκνία, καὶ νενικήκατε[6] αὐτούς, ὅτι μείζων ἐστὶν ὁ ἐν ὑμῖν ἢ ὁ ἐν τῷ κόσμῳ. **5.** αὐτοὶ ἐκ τοῦ κόσμου εἰσίν· διὰ τοῦτο ἐκ τοῦ κόσμου λαλοῦσιν καὶ ὁ κόσμος αὐτῶν[7] ἀκούει. **6.** ἡμεῖς ἐκ τοῦ θεοῦ ἐσμεν· ὁ γινώσκων τὸν θεὸν ἀκούει ἡμῶν, ὃς οὐκ ἔστιν ἐκ τοῦ θεοῦ οὐκ ἀκούει ἡμῶν. ἐκ τούτου γινώσκομεν τὸ πνεῦμα τῆς ἀληθείας καὶ τὸ πνεῦμα τῆς πλάνης.[8]

Parsing:　ἐξεληλύθασιν ....

　　　　　　ἐληλυθότα ....

　　　　　　ἀκηκόατε ....

Translation: ....

....

....

....

....

....

....

....

....

....

....

....

....

....

---

[3]δοκιμάζω, *I examine, test, approve* [Vocab. 11].　　[4]ψευδοπροφήτης, -ου, ὁ, *false prophet* (11).
[5]ἀντίχριστος, -ου, ὁ, *Antichrist* (5).　　[6]νικάω, *I overcome, conquer, prevail* [Vocab. 8].　　[7]What is the case of this word? Why?　　[8]πλάνη, -ης, ἡ, *deception, wandering, error* (10).

Reading 3 | 1 John 4:7–11

7. Ἀγαπητοί, ἀγαπῶμεν ἀλλήλους, ὅτι ἡ ἀγάπη ἐκ τοῦ θεοῦ ἐστιν, καὶ πᾶς ὁ ἀγαπῶν ἐκ τοῦ θεοῦ γεγέννηται καὶ γινώσκει τὸν θεόν. **8.** ὁ μὴ ἀγαπῶν οὐκ ἔγνω τὸν θεόν, ὅτι ὁ θεὸς ἀγάπη ἐστίν. **9.** ἐν τούτῳ ἐφανερώθη[9] ἡ ἀγάπη τοῦ θεοῦ ἐν ἡμῖν, ὅτι τὸν υἱὸν αὐτοῦ τὸν μονογενῆ[10] ἀπέσταλκεν ὁ θεὸς εἰς τὸν κόσμον ἵνα ζήσωμεν δι᾽ αὐτοῦ. **10.** ἐν τούτῳ ἐστὶν ἡ ἀγάπη, οὐχ ὅτι ἡμεῖς ἠγαπήκαμεν τὸν θεόν, ἀλλ᾽ ὅτι αὐτὸς ἠγάπησεν ἡμᾶς καὶ ἀπέστειλεν τὸν υἱὸν αὐτοῦ ἱλασμὸν[11] περὶ τῶν ἁμαρτιῶν ἡμῶν. **11.** Ἀγαπητοί, εἰ οὕτως ὁ θεὸς ἠγάπησεν ἡμᾶς, καὶ ἡμεῖς ὀφείλομεν[12] ἀλλήλους ἀγαπᾶν.

Parsing: ἀγαπητοί _____

ἠγαπήκαμεν _____

ἀγαπᾶν _____

Translation: _____

_____

_____

_____

_____

_____

_____

_____

_____

_____

_____

_____

_____

_____

_____

_____

_____

---

[9]φανερόω, _I reveal, make known_ [Vocab. 2].   [10]μονογενής, -ές, _unique, one and only, only begotten_ (9).
[11]ἱλασμός, -οῦ, ὁ, _atoning sacrifice_ (2).   [12]ὀφείλω, _I owe, ought_ [Vocab. 5].

Reading 4 | 1 John 4:12–16a

12. θεὸν οὐδεὶς πώποτε[13] τεθέαται.[14] ἐὰν ἀγαπῶμεν ἀλλήλους, ὁ θεὸς ἐν ἡμῖν μένει καὶ ἡ ἀγάπη αὐτοῦ ἐν ἡμῖν τετελειωμένη[15] ἐστίν.

13. Ἐν τούτῳ γινώσκομεν ὅτι ἐν αὐτῷ μένομεν καὶ αὐτὸς ἐν ἡμῖν, ὅτι ἐκ τοῦ πνεύματος αὐτοῦ <u>δέδωκεν</u> ἡμῖν. **14.** καὶ ἡμεῖς τεθεάμεθα καὶ <u>μαρτυροῦμεν</u> ὅτι ὁ πατὴρ ἀπέσταλκεν τὸν υἱὸν σωτῆρα[16] τοῦ κόσμου. **15.** ὃς ἐὰν ὁμολογήσῃ[17] ὅτι Ἰησοῦς ἐστιν ὁ υἱὸς τοῦ θεοῦ, ὁ θεὸς ἐν αὐτῷ μένει καὶ αὐτὸς ἐν τῷ θεῷ. **16.** καὶ ἡμεῖς ἐγνώκαμεν καὶ πεπιστεύκαμεν τὴν ἀγάπην <u>ἣν</u> ἔχει ὁ θεὸς ἐν ἡμῖν.

Parsing: δέδωκεν _____

            μαρτυροῦμεν _____

            ἣν _____

Translation: _____

_____

_____

_____

_____

_____

_____

_____

_____

_____

_____

_____

_____

_____

_____

_____

---

[13]πώποτε, *ever, at any time* (6).   [14]θεάομαι, *I see, look at* [Vocab. 11].   [15]τελειόω, *I fulfill, make perfect* [Vocab. 10].   [16]σωτήρ, -ῆρος, ὁ, *Savior* [Vocab. 10].   [17]ὁμολογέω, *I confess, profess* [Vocab. 9].

Reading 5 | **1 John 4:16b–21**

Ὁ θεὸς ἀγάπη ἐστίν, καὶ ὁ μένων ἐν τῇ ἀγάπῃ ἐν τῷ θεῷ μένει καὶ ὁ θεὸς ἐν αὐτῷ μένει.

17. ἐν τούτῳ τετελείωται[18] ἡ ἀγάπη μεθ᾽ ἡμῶν, ἵνα παρρησίαν[19] ἔχωμεν ἐν τῇ ἡμέρᾳ τῆς κρίσεως, ὅτι καθὼς ἐκεῖνός ἐστιν καὶ ἡμεῖς ἐσμεν ἐν τῷ κόσμῳ τούτῳ. **18.** φόβος οὐκ ἔστιν ἐν τῇ ἀγάπῃ, ἀλλ᾽ ἡ τελεία[20] ἀγάπη ἔξω βάλλει τὸν φόβον, ὅτι ὁ φόβος κόλασιν[21] ἔχει, ὁ δὲ φοβούμενος οὐ τετελείωται ἐν τῇ ἀγάπῃ.

19. ἡμεῖς ἀγαπῶμεν, ὅτι αὐτὸς πρῶτος ἠγάπησεν ἡμᾶς. **20.** ἐάν τις εἴπῃ ὅτι Ἀγαπῶ τὸν θεόν, καὶ τὸν ἀδελφὸν αὐτοῦ μισῇ,[22] ψεύστης[23] ἐστίν· ὁ γὰρ μὴ ἀγαπῶν τὸν ἀδελφὸν αὐτοῦ ὃν ἑώρακεν, τὸν θεὸν ὃν οὐχ ἑώρακεν οὐ δύναται ἀγαπᾶν. **21.** καὶ ταύτην τὴν ἐντολὴν ἔχομεν ἀπ᾽ αὐτοῦ, ἵνα ὁ ἀγαπῶν τὸν θεὸν ἀγαπᾷ καὶ τὸν ἀδελφὸν αὐτοῦ.

Parsing: κρίσεως _____

ἔξω _____

ἀγαπᾷ _____

Translation: _____

_____

_____

_____

_____

_____

_____

_____

_____

_____

_____

_____

_____

_____

_____

_____

_____

[18]See 4:12, above.   [19]παρρησία, -ας, ἡ, *boldness, confidence* [Vocab. 6].   [20]τέλειος, -α, -ον, *complete, perfect* (19).
[21]κόλασις, -εως, ἡ, *punishment* (2).   [22]μισέω, *I hate, detest* [Vocab. 4].   [23]ψεύστης, -ου, ὁ, *liar* (10).

Reading 6 | 1 John 5:1–6

1. Πᾶς ὁ πιστεύων ὅτι Ἰησοῦς ἐστιν ὁ Χριστός ἐκ τοῦ θεοῦ γεγέννηται, καὶ πᾶς ὁ ἀγαπῶν τὸν γεννήσαντα ἀγαπᾷ [καὶ] τὸν <u>γεγεννημένον</u> ἐξ αὐτοῦ. **2.** ἐν τούτῳ γινώσκομεν ὅτι ἀγαπῶμεν τὰ τέκνα τοῦ θεοῦ, ὅταν τὸν θεὸν ἀγαπῶμεν καὶ τὰς ἐντολὰς αὐτοῦ ποιῶμεν. **3.** αὕτη γάρ ἐστιν ἡ ἀγάπη τοῦ θεοῦ, ἵνα τὰς ἐντολὰς αὐτοῦ τηρῶμεν· καὶ αἱ ἐντολαὶ αὐτοῦ βαρεῖαι[24] οὐκ εἰσίν, **4.** ὅτι πᾶν τὸ γεγεννημένον ἐκ τοῦ θεοῦ νικᾷ[25] τὸν κόσμον· καὶ αὕτη ἐστὶν ἡ νίκη[26] ἡ νικήσασα τὸν κόσμον, ἡ πίστις ἡμῶν. **5.** τίς δέ ἐστιν ὁ νικῶν τὸν κόσμον εἰ μὴ ὁ πιστεύων ὅτι Ἰησοῦς ἐστιν ὁ υἱὸς τοῦ θεοῦ·

6. Οὗτός ἐστιν ὁ ἐλθὼν δι᾽ ὕδατος καὶ αἵματος, Ἰησοῦς Χριστός, οὐκ ἐν τῷ ὕδατι μόνον ἀλλ᾽ ἐν τῷ <u>ὕδατι</u> καὶ ἐν τῷ αἵματι· καὶ τὸ πνεῦμά ἐστιν τὸ <u>μαρτυροῦν</u>, ὅτι τὸ πνεῦμά ἐστιν ἡ ἀλήθεια.

Parsing: γεγεννημένον _____
          ὕδατι _____
          μαρτυροῦν _____

Translation: _____

_____

_____

_____

_____

_____

_____

_____

_____

_____

_____

---

[24]βαρύς, -εῖα, -ύ, *burdensome, oppressive* (6).   [25]νικάω, see 4:4, above.   [26]νίκη, -ης, ἡ, *victory* (1).

Week Two
John 16:1–33

Reading 1 | **John 16:1–6**

1. Ταῦτα λελάληκα ὑμῖν ἵνα μὴ σκανδαλισθῆτε.[1] **2.** ἀποσυναγώγους[2] <u>ποιήσουσιν</u> ὑμᾶς· ἀλλ᾽ ἔρχεται ὥρα ἵνα πᾶς ὁ ἀποκτείνας ὑμᾶς <u>δόξῃ</u> λατρείαν[3] προσφέρειν τῷ θεῷ. **3.** καὶ ταῦτα ποιήσουσιν ὅτι οὐκ ἔγνωσαν τὸν πατέρα οὐδὲ ἐμέ. **4.** ἀλλὰ ταῦτα λελάληκα ὑμῖν ἵνα ὅταν ἔλθῃ ἡ ὥρα μνημονεύητε[4] ὅτι ἐγὼ εἶπον ὑμῖν.

Ταῦτα δὲ ὑμῖν ἐξ ἀρχῆς οὐκ εἶπον, ὅτι μεθ᾽ ὑμῶν <u>ἤμην</u>. **5.** νῦν δὲ ὑπάγω πρὸς τὸν πέμψαντά με, καὶ οὐδεὶς ἐξ ὑμῶν <u>ἐρωτᾷ</u> με, Ποῦ ὑπάγεις; **6.** ἀλλ᾽ ὅτι ταῦτα λελάληκα ὑμῖν ἡ λύπη[5] πεπλήρωκεν ὑμῶν τὴν καρδίαν.

Parsing:
- ποιήσουσιν _____
- δόξῃ _____
- ἤμην _____
- ἐρωτᾷ _____

Translation:

_____

_____

_____

_____

_____

_____

_____

_____

_____

_____

_____

---

[1]σκανδαλίζω, *I stumble, cause to fall, take offense (pass)* [Vocab. 7].   [2]ἀποσυνάγωγος, -ον, *expelled from the synagogue* (3).   [3]λατρεία, -ας, ἡ, *service, religious service* (3).   [4]μνημονεύω, *I remember, recall, recollect* [Vocab. 12]. This verb can take an object in either the accusative or genitive case (BAGD; s.v. μνημονεύω, 1.a; 1.b).   [5]λύπη, -ης, ἡ, *grief, sorrow, pain* (16).

19

Reading 2 | John 16:7–11

7. ἀλλ᾽ ἐγὼ τὴν ἀλήθειαν λέγω ὑμῖν, συμφέρει⁶ ὑμῖν ἵνα ἐγὼ ἀπέλθω. ἐὰν γὰρ μὴ ἀπέλθω, ὁ παράκλητος⁷ οὐκ <u>ἐλεύσεται</u> πρὸς ὑμᾶς· ἐὰν δὲ πορευθῶ, πέμψω αὐτὸν πρὸς ὑμᾶς. **8.** καὶ <u>ἐλθὼν</u> ἐκεῖνος ἐλέγξει⁸ τὸν κόσμον περὶ ἁμαρτίας καὶ περὶ δικαιοσύνης καὶ περὶ κρίσεως· **9.** περὶ ἁμαρτίας μέν, ὅτι οὐ πιστεύουσιν εἰς <u>ἐμέ</u>· **10.** περὶ δικαιοσύνης δέ, ὅτι πρὸς τὸν πατέρα ὑπάγω καὶ οὐκέτι θεωρεῖτέ με· **11.** περὶ δὲ κρίσεως, ὅτι ὁ ἄρχων τοῦ κόσμου τούτου κέκριται.

Parsing: ἐλεύσεται _____

ἐλθὼν _____

ἐμέ _____

Translation: _____

_____

_____

_____

_____

_____

_____

_____

_____

_____

_____

_____

_____

_____

_____

_____

_____

_____

_____

---

⁶συμφέρω, *I bring together, it is good* (15).   ⁷παράκλητος, -ου, ὁ, *advocate, helper, intercessor* (5).   ⁸ἐλέγχω, *I convict, expose, convince, reprove* (17).

Reading 3 | John 16:12–16

12. Ἔτι πολλὰ ἔχω ὑμῖν λέγειν, ἀλλ᾽ οὐ δύνασθε βαστάζειν[9] ἄρτι· **13.** ὅταν δὲ ἔλθῃ ἐκεῖνος, τὸ πνεῦμα τῆς ἀληθείας, ὁδηγήσει[10] ὑμᾶς ἐν τῇ ἀληθείᾳ πάσῃ· οὐ γὰρ λαλήσει ἀφ᾽ ἑαυτοῦ, ἀλλ᾽ ὅσα <u>ἀκούσει</u> λαλήσει, καὶ τὰ ἐρχόμενα ἀναγγελεῖ[11] ὑμῖν. **14.** ἐκεῖνος ἐμὲ δοξάσει, ὅτι ἐκ τοῦ ἐμοῦ <u>λήμψεται</u> καὶ ἀναγγελεῖ ὑμῖν. **15.** πάντα ὅσα ἔχει ὁ πατὴρ ἐμά ἐστιν· διὰ τοῦτο εἶπον ὅτι ἐκ τοῦ ἐμοῦ λαμβάνει καὶ ἀναγγελεῖ ὑμῖν.

16. Μικρὸν καὶ οὐκέτι θεωρεῖτέ με, καὶ πάλιν μικρὸν καὶ <u>ὄψεσθε</u> με.

Parsing: ἀκούσει _____

             λήμψεται _____

             ὄψεσθε _____

Translation: _____

---

[9]βαστάζω, *I bear, endure, carry, comprehend* [Vocab. 8].   [10]ὁδηγέω, *I lead, guide* (5).   [11]ἀναγγέλλω, *I report, announce* (14).

Reading 4 | John 16:17–22

17. εἶπαν οὖν ἐκ[12] τῶν μαθητῶν αὐτοῦ πρὸς ἀλλήλους, Τί ἐστιν τοῦτο ὃ λέγει ἡμῖν, Μικρὸν καὶ οὐ θεωρεῖτέ με, καὶ πάλιν μικρὸν καὶ ὄψεσθέ με; καί, Ὅτι ὑπάγω πρὸς τὸν πατέρα; **18.** ἔλεγον οὖν, Τί ἐστιν τοῦτο, ὃ λέγει, τὸ μικρόν· οὐκ οἴδαμεν τί λαλεῖ.

19. ἔγνω ὁ Ἰησοῦς ὅτι ἤθελον αὐτὸν ἐρωτᾶν, καὶ εἶπεν αὐτοῖς, Περὶ τούτου ζητεῖτε μετ' ἀλλήλων ὅτι εἶπον, Μικρὸν καὶ οὐ θεωρεῖτέ με, καὶ πάλιν μικρὸν καὶ ὄψεσθέ με; **20.** ἀμὴν ἀμὴν λέγω ὑμῖν ὅτι κλαύσετε[13] καὶ θρηνήσετε[14] ὑμεῖς, ὁ δὲ κόσμος χαρήσεται· ὑμεῖς λυπηθήσεσθε[15] ἀλλ' ἡ λύπη[16] ὑμῶν εἰς χαρὰν γενήσεται. **21.** ἡ γυνὴ ὅταν τίκτῃ[17] λύπην ἔχει, ὅτι ἦλθεν ἡ ὥρα αὐτῆς· ὅταν δὲ γεννήσῃ τὸ παιδίον, οὐκέτι μνημονεύει[18] τῆς θλίψεως διὰ τὴν χαρὰν ὅτι ἐγεννήθη ἄνθρωπος εἰς τὸν κόσμον. **22.** καὶ ὑμεῖς οὖν νῦν μὲν λύπην ἔχετε· πάλιν δὲ ὄψομαι ὑμᾶς, καὶ χαρήσεται ὑμῶν ἡ καρδία, καὶ τὴν χαρὰν ὑμῶν οὐδεὶς αἴρει ἀφ' ὑμῶν.

Parsing:　　ἔγνω　..

　　　　　　　ἤθελον　..

　　　　　　　χαρήσεται　..

Translation:

....

....

....

....

....

....

....

....

....

....

....

....

....

[12]The preposition is being used partitively, that is, to express a part of a whole group. The whole group is the subject of the main verb (Wallace, 85; 371).　　[13]κλαίω, *I weep, cry* [Vocab. 4].　　[14]θρηνέω, *I lament* (4).　　[15]λυπέω, *I grieve, pain* [Vocab. 8].　　[16]See verse 6.　　[17]τίκτω, *I give birth* (17).　　[18]See verse 4.

Reading 5 | John 16:23–27

23. καὶ ἐν ἐκείνῃ τῇ ἡμέρᾳ ἐμὲ οὐκ <u>ἐρωτήσετε</u> οὐδέν. ἀμὴν ἀμὴν λέγω ὑμῖν, ἄν τι αἰτήσητε τὸν πατέρα ἐν τῷ ὀνόματί μου <u>δώσει</u> ὑμῖν. **24.** ἕως ἄρτι οὐκ ᾐτήσατε οὐδὲν ἐν τῷ ὀνόματί μου· αἰτεῖτε καὶ λήμψεσθε, ἵνα ἡ χαρὰ ὑμῶν <u>ᾖ</u> πεπληρωμένη.

25. Ταῦτα ἐν παροιμίαις[19] λελάληκα ὑμῖν· ἔρχεται ὥρα ὅτε οὐκέτι ἐν παροιμίαις λαλήσω ὑμῖν ἀλλὰ παρρησίᾳ[20] περὶ τοῦ πατρὸς ἀπαγγελῶ ὑμῖν. **26.** ἐν ἐκείνῃ τῇ ἡμέρᾳ ἐν τῷ ὀνόματί μου αἰτήσεσθε, καὶ οὐ λέγω ὑμῖν ὅτι ἐγὼ ἐρωτήσω τὸν πατέρα περὶ ὑμῶν· **27.** αὐτὸς γὰρ ὁ πατὴρ φιλεῖ[21] ὑμᾶς, ὅτι ὑμεῖς ἐμὲ πεφιλήκατε καὶ πεπιστεύκατε ὅτι ἐγὼ παρὰ τοῦ θεοῦ ἐξῆλθον.

Parsing: ἐρωτήσετε _____

δώσει _____

ᾖ _____

Translation: _____

_____

_____

_____

_____

_____

_____

_____

_____

_____

_____

_____

_____

_____

_____

_____

[19]παροιμία, -ας, ἡ, *parable, proverb, figure of speech* (5). [20]παρρησία, -ας, ἡ, *boldness, confidence* [Vocab. 6].
[21]φιλέω, *I love, like, kiss* [Vocab. 9].

Reading 6 | John 16:28–33

28. ἐξῆλθον παρὰ τοῦ πατρὸς καὶ ἐλήλυθα εἰς τὸν κόσμον· πάλιν ἀφίημι τὸν κόσμον καὶ πορεύομαι πρὸς τὸν πατέρα. **29.** Λέγουσιν οἱ μαθηταὶ αὐτοῦ, Ἴδε νῦν ἐν παρρησίᾳ[22] λαλεῖς, καὶ παροιμίαν[23] οὐδεμίαν λέγεις. **30.** νῦν οἴδαμεν ὅτι οἶδας πάντα καὶ οὐ χρείαν ἔχεις ἵνα τίς σε <u>ἐρωτᾷ</u>· ἐν τούτῳ πιστεύομεν ὅτι ἀπὸ θεοῦ ἐξῆλθες.

31. ἀπεκρίθη αὐτοῖς Ἰησοῦς, Ἄρτι πιστεύετε; **32.** ἰδοὺ ἔρχεται ὥρα καὶ <u>ἐλήλυθεν</u> ἵνα σκορπισθῆτε[24] ἕκαστος εἰς τὰ ἴδια κἀμὲ[25] μόνον <u>ἀφῆτε</u>· καὶ οὐκ εἰμὶ μόνος, ὅτι ὁ πατὴρ μετ᾿ ἐμοῦ ἐστιν.

33. ταῦτα λελάληκα ὑμῖν ἵνα ἐν ἐμοὶ εἰρήνην ἔχητε· ἐν τῷ κόσμῳ θλῖψιν ἔχετε, ἀλλὰ θαρσεῖτε,[26] ἐγὼ νενίκηκα[27] τὸν κόσμον.

Parsing: ἐρωτᾷ _____

ἐλήλυθεν _____

ἀφῆτε _____

Translation: _____

_____

_____

_____

_____

_____

_____

_____

_____

_____

_____

_____

_____

_____

_____

_____

[22]See verse 25.   [23]See verse 25.   [24]σκορπίζω, *I disperse, scatter* (5).   [25]καὶ + ἐμέ, *and me* (3).
[26]θαρσέω, *I am of good cheer, I am confident* (7).   [27]νικάω, *I overcome, conquer, prevail* [Vocab. 8].

Vocabulary

Friends	Memory Aids
ἀποδίδωμι, *I give away, give up, pay* (48).	I *give* (δίδωμι) *away* (ἀπό).
ἐπιγινώσκω, *I know, understand, recognize* (44).	I *know* (γινώσκω) by looking upon (ἐπί).
μικρός, -ά, -όν, *small, humble, little* (46).	Micro—*small*.
παραλαμβάνω, *I take, take along, receive* (49).	I *take* (λαμβάνω) from (παρά).
ποῦ, *where?* (48).	ὅπου—*where*.
προσφέρω, *I bring to, offer* (47).	I carry (φέρω) to (πρός).
φόβος, -ου, ὁ, *fear, terror* (47).	Phobia—*fear*.

Cousins	
ἁμαρτωλός, -όν, *sinful, sinner* (47).	ἁμαρτία—sin.
ἀπαγγέλλω, *I report, announce* (45).	A messenger (ἄγγελος) *reports*.
ἔρημος, -ον, *abandoned, desolate, desert, wilderness* (48).	Hermits (*eremites*) live in the *desert*.
καθίζω, *I cause to sit down, appoint* (46).	*Down* (κατά, καθ').
ὅμοιος, -οία, -οιον, *of the same nature, like* (45).	Homo—*same*.
οὐκέτι, *no longer, no more* (47).	Not (οὐ) yet (ἔτι).
πρό, *before, in front of, at* (47).	I am an amateur *before* I turn *pro*.
σωτηρία, -ας, ἡ, *salvation, deliverance* (46).	Soteriology—spiritual *salvation*.

Strangers	
ἄρα, *so, then, consequently* (49).	*So, then* I was bitten by an <u>ar</u>achnid (spider).
ἄχρι, ἄχρις, *until, to, as far as* (49).	His sister was <u>acri</u>monious *until* she married.
διώκω, *I hasten, pursue, persecute* (45).	
ἔμπροσθεν, *in front of, before* (48).	Related to πρό (see Cousins, above).
ἔτος, -ους, τό, *year* (49).	
θηρίον, -ου, τό, *animal, beast, snake* (46).	<u>Ther</u>ianthropic—part human, part *animal*.
θλῖψις, -εως, ἡ, *oppression, tribulation* (45).	
κρατέω, *I grasp, attain, hold fast* (47).	Flee the *grasp* of the <u>Kra</u>ken (sea monster).
κρίσις, -εως, ἡ, *judging, judgment, condemnation* (47).	A <u>cris</u>is requires *judgment*.
ναός, -οῦ, ὁ, *temple, sanctuary* (45).	The people (λαός) go to the *temple* (ναός).
οὐαί, *woe, alas* (46).	A cry of pain.
σταυρόω, *I crucify* (46).	
φανερόω, *I reveal, make known* (49).	The <u>phan</u>tom will be *revealed*.
φυλακή, -ῆς, ἡ, *watch, guard, prison* (47).	A <u>phyla</u>ctery *guards* one's thoughts.
χρεία, -ας, ἡ, *need, necessity, lack* (49).	I have a χρεία-tical (critical) *need*.

Week Three
Matthew 16:13–17:16

Reading 1 │ Matthew 16:13–17

13. Ἐλθὼν δὲ ὁ Ἰησοῦς εἰς τὰ <u>μέρη</u> Καισαρείας τῆς Φιλίππου <u>ἠρώτα</u> τοὺς μαθητὰς αὐτοῦ λέγων, Τίνα λέγουσιν οἱ ἄνθρωποι εἶναι τὸν υἱὸν τοῦ ἀνθρώπου;

14. οἱ δὲ εἶπαν, Οἱ μὲν Ἰωάννην τὸν βαπτιστήν,[1] ἄλλοι δὲ Ἠλίαν,[2] ἕτεροι δὲ Ἰερεμίαν[3] ἢ <u>ἕνα</u> τῶν προφητῶν.

15. λέγει αὐτοῖς, Ὑμεῖς[4] δὲ τίνα με λέγετε εἶναι;

16. ἀποκριθεὶς δὲ Σίμων Πέτρος εἶπεν, Σὺ εἶ ὁ Χριστὸς ὁ υἱὸς τοῦ θεοῦ τοῦ ζῶντος.

17. ἀποκριθεὶς δὲ ὁ Ἰησοῦς εἶπεν αὐτῷ, Μακάριος εἶ, Σίμων Βαριωνᾶ,[5] ὅτι σὰρξ καὶ αἷμα οὐκ ἀπεκάλυψεν[6] σοι ἀλλ᾽ ὁ πατήρ μου ὁ ἐν τοῖς οὐρανοῖς.

Parsing: μέρη _____

             ἠρώτα _____

             ἕνα _____

Translation: _____

_____

_____

_____

_____

_____

_____

_____

_____

_____

_____

---

[1]βαπτιστής, -οῦ, ὁ, *Baptist, Baptizer* (12).   [2]Ἠλίας, -ου, ὁ, *Elijah* [Vocab. 7].   [3]Ἰερεμίας, -ου, ὁ, *Jeremiah* (3).   [4]Here is an example of a pronoun that has been pushed to the front of the sentence to convey emphasis (*BBG*, 86; Wallace, 321).   [5]Βαριωνᾶ, ὁ, *Bar-Jona, Son of Jonah* (1).   [6]ἀποκαλύπτω, *I reveal, uncover* [Vocab. 8].

Reading 2 | Matthew 16:18–22

18. κἀγὼ δέ σοι λέγω ὅτι σὺ εἶ Πέτρος, καὶ ἐπὶ ταύτη τῇ πέτρᾳ[7] οἰκοδομήσω[8] μου τὴν ἐκκλησίαν, καὶ πύλαι[9] ᾅδου[10] οὐ κατισχύσουσιν[11] αὐτῆς. **19.** <u>δώσω</u> σοι τὰς κλεῖδας[12] τῆς βασιλείας τῶν οὐρανῶν, καὶ ὃ ἐὰν <u>δήσῃς</u> ἐπὶ τῆς γῆς ἔσται δεδεμένον ἐν τοῖς οὐρανοῖς, καὶ ὃ ἐὰν λύσῃς ἐπὶ τῆς γῆς ἔσται λελυμένον ἐν τοῖς οὐρανοῖς. **20.** τότε ἐπετίμησεν[13] τοῖς μαθηταῖς ἵνα μηδενὶ εἴπωσιν ὅτι αὐτός ἐστιν ὁ Χριστός.

21. Ἀπὸ τότε <u>ἤρξατο</u> ὁ Ἰησοῦς δεικνύειν[14] τοῖς μαθηταῖς αὐτοῦ ὅτι δεῖ αὐτὸν εἰς Ἱεροσόλυμα ἀπελθεῖν καὶ πολλὰ παθεῖν ἀπὸ τῶν πρεσβυτέρων καὶ ἀρχιερέων καὶ γραμματέων καὶ ἀποκτανθῆναι καὶ τῇ τρίτῃ ἡμέρᾳ ἐγερθῆναι.

22. καὶ προσλαβόμενος[15] αὐτὸν ὁ Πέτρος ἤρξατο ἐπιτιμᾶν[16] αὐτῷ λέγων, Ἵλεώς[17] σοι, κύριε· οὐ μὴ ἔσται σοι τοῦτο.

Parsing: δώσω   _____

δήσῃς   _____

ἤρξατο   _____

Translation: _____

_____

_____

_____

_____

_____

_____

_____

_____

_____

_____

_____

---

[7]πέτρα, -ας, ἡ, *rock* (15).   [8]οἰκοδομέω, *I build, edify* [Vocab. 4].   [9]πύλη, -ης, ἡ, *gate, door* (10). [10]ᾅδης, -ου, ὁ, *Hades, hell* (10).   [11]κατισχύω, *I prevail, overpower* (3).   [12]κλείς, κλειδός, ἡ, *key* (6). [13]ἐπιτιμάω, *I rebuke, warn* [Vocab. 7].   [14]δείκνυμι, *I show, explain* [Vocab. 5].   [15]προσλαμβάνω, *I take aside* (12).   [16]ἐπιτιμάω, *I rebuke, warn* [Vocab. 7].   [17]ἵλεως, -ων, *gracious, merciful* (2). *Gracious to you* does not make much sense in this context. Ἵλεως appears in the Septuagint (2 Kings 23:17; 1 Chron. 11:19; Isa. 54:10) as well as Heb. 8:12. In our translation, we have used *God forbid!* (BAGD, s.v. ἵλεως).

Reading 3	Matthew 16:23–28

23. ὁ δὲ στραφεὶς[18] εἶπεν τῷ Πέτρῳ, Ὕπαγε ὀπίσω[19] μου, Σατανᾶ· σκάνδαλον[20] εἶ ἐμοῦ,

ὅτι οὐ φρονεῖς[21] τὰ τοῦ θεοῦ ἀλλὰ τὰ τῶν ἀνθρώπων.

24. Τότε ὁ Ἰησοῦς εἶπεν τοῖς μαθηταῖς αὐτοῦ, Εἴ τις θέλει ὀπίσω μου ἐλθεῖν,

ἀπαρνησάσθω[22] ἑαυτὸν καὶ ἀράτω τὸν σταυρὸν[23] αὐτοῦ καὶ ἀκολουθείτω μοι. **25.** ὃς γὰρ ἐὰν

θέλῃ τὴν ψυχὴν αὐτοῦ σῶσαι ἀπολέσει αὐτήν· ὃς δ᾽ ἂν ἀπολέσῃ τὴν ψυχὴν αὐτοῦ ἕνεκεν[24]

ἐμοῦ εὑρήσει αὐτήν. **26.** τί γὰρ ὠφεληθήσεται[25] ἄνθρωπος ἐὰν τὸν κόσμον ὅλον κερδήσῃ[26]

τὴν δὲ ψυχὴν αὐτοῦ ζημιωθῇ;[27] ἢ τί δώσει ἄνθρωπος ἀντάλλαγμα[28] τῆς ψυχῆς αὐτοῦ;

27. μέλλει γὰρ ὁ υἱὸς τοῦ ἀνθρώπου ἔρχεσθαι ἐν τῇ δόξῃ τοῦ πατρὸς αὐτοῦ μετὰ τῶν

ἀγγέλων αὐτοῦ, καὶ τότε ἀποδώσει ἑκάστῳ κατὰ τὴν πρᾶξιν[29] αὐτοῦ. **28.** ἀμὴν λέγω ὑμῖν ὅτι

εἰσίν τινες τῶν ὧδε ἑστώτων οἵτινες οὐ μὴ γεύσωνται[30] θανάτου ἕως ἂν ἴδωσιν τὸν υἱὸν τοῦ

ἀνθρώπου ἐρχόμενον ἐν τῇ βασιλείᾳ αὐτοῦ.

Parsing: εἶ   _____

               σῶσαι _____

               ἴδωσιν _____

Translation:

---

[18]στρέφω, *I turn, change, return* [Vocab. 5].   [19]ὀπίσω, *behind, after* [Vocab. 5].   [20]σκάνδαλον, -ου, τό, *trap, temptation, stumbling block* (15).   [21]φρονέω, *I think* [Vocab. 9].   [22]ἀπαρνέομαι, *I deny* (12).   [23]σταυρός, -οῦ, ὁ, *cross* [Vocab. 8].   [24]ἕνεκα, *because of, on account of* [Vocab. 8].   [25]ὠφελέω, *I help, gain* (15). [26]κερδαίνω, *I gain, profit* (17).   [27]ζημιόω, *I forfeit, suffer damage or loss* (6). This verb only occurs in the passive voice in our literature (BAGD, s.v. ζημιόω).   [28]ἀντάλλαγμα, -ατος, τό, *something given in exchange* (2). [29]πρᾶξις, -εως, ἡ, *conduct, work, deed,* (6).   [30]γεύομαι, *I taste, partake of, eat* (15).

Reading 4 | Matthew 17:1–5

1. Καὶ μεθ᾽ ἡμέρας ἓξ παραλαμβάνει ὁ Ἰησοῦς τὸν Πέτρον καὶ Ἰάκωβον καὶ Ἰωάννην τὸν ἀδελφὸν αὐτοῦ καὶ ἀναφέρει[31] αὐτοὺς εἰς ὄρος ὑψηλὸν[32] κατ᾽ ἰδίαν.[33]

2. καὶ μετεμορφώθη[34] ἔμπροσθεν αὐτῶν, καὶ ἔλαμψεν[35] τὸ πρόσωπον αὐτοῦ ὡς ὁ ἥλιος,[36] τὰ δὲ ἱμάτια αὐτοῦ ἐγένετο λευκὰ[37] ὡς τὸ φῶς. **3.** καὶ ἰδοὺ <u>ὤφθη</u> αὐτοῖς Μωϋσῆς καὶ Ἠλίας[38] συλλαλοῦντες[39] μετ᾽ αὐτοῦ.

4. ἀποκριθεὶς δὲ ὁ Πέτρος εἶπεν τῷ Ἰησοῦ, Κύριε, καλόν ἐστιν ἡμᾶς ὧδε εἶναι· εἰ θέλεις, ποιήσω ὧδε τρεῖς σκηνάς,[40] σοὶ <u>μίαν</u> καὶ Μωϋσεῖ μίαν καὶ Ἠλίᾳ μίαν.

5. ἔτι αὐτοῦ λαλοῦντος ἰδοὺ νεφέλη[41] φωτεινὴ[42] ἐπεσκίασεν[43] αὐτούς, καὶ ἰδοὺ φωνὴ ἐκ τῆς νεφέλης λέγουσα, Οὗτός ἐστιν ὁ υἱός μου ὁ ἀγαπητός, ἐν <u>ᾧ</u> εὐδόκησα·[44] ἀκούετε αὐτοῦ.

Parsing: ὤφθη _____

μίαν _____

ᾧ _____

Translation:

_____

_____

_____

_____

_____

_____

_____

_____

_____

_____

_____

_____

_____

_____

[31]ἀναφέρω, *I bring up, take up* (10). [32]ὑψηλός, -ή, -όν, *high, exalted* (11). [33]κατ᾽ ἰδίαν, *privately* (BAGD, s.v. ἴδιος, 4). [34]μεταμορφόω, *I am transformed, changed* (4). [35]λάμπω, *I shine* (7). [36]ἥλιος, -ου, ὁ, *sun* [Vocab. 6]. [37]λευκός, -ή, -όν, *white, bright* [Vocab. 9]. [38]See verse 14. [39]συλλαλέω, *I talk, discuss* (6). [40]σκῆνος, -ους, τό, *tent, shelter* (2). [41]νεφέλη, -ης, ἡ, *cloud* [Vocab 9]. [42]φωτεινός, -ή, -όν, *bright, radiant* (2). [43]ἐπισκιάζω, *I overshadow* (5). [44]εὐδοκέω, *I am well pleased, content* [Vocab. 11].

Reading 5 | Matthew 17:6–10

6. καὶ ἀκούσαντες οἱ μαθηταὶ <u>ἔπεσαν</u> ἐπὶ πρόσωπον αὐτῶν καὶ <u>ἐφοβήθησαν</u> σφόδρα.[45]

7. καὶ προσῆλθεν ὁ Ἰησοῦς καὶ ἁψάμενος[46] αὐτῶν εἶπεν, Ἐγέρθητε καὶ μὴ φοβεῖσθε.

8. ἐπάραντες[47] δὲ τοὺς ὀφθαλμοὺς αὐτῶν οὐδένα εἶδον εἰ μὴ αὐτὸν Ἰησοῦν μόνον.

9. Καὶ καταβαινόντων αὐτῶν ἐκ τοῦ ὄρους ἐνετείλατο[48] αὐτοῖς ὁ Ἰησοῦς λέγων, <u>Μηδενὶ</u> εἴπητε τὸ ὅραμα[49] ἕως οὗ[50] ὁ υἱὸς τοῦ ἀνθρώπου ἐκ νεκρῶν ἐγερθῇ.

10. καὶ ἐπηρώτησαν αὐτὸν οἱ μαθηταὶ λέγοντες, Τί οὖν οἱ γραμματεῖς λέγουσιν ὅτι Ἡλίαν[51] δεῖ ἐλθεῖν πρῶτον;

Parsing: ἔπεσαν   ....

ἐφοβήθησαν   ....

μηδενὶ   ....

Translation: ....

....

....

....

....

....

....

....

....

....

....

....

....

....

....

....

....

....

....

---

[45]σφόδρα, *extremely, greatly* (11).   [46]ἅπτομαι, *I touch* [Vocab. 4].   [47]ἐπαίρω, *I lift up, raise* (19) (BAGD, s.v. ἐπαίρω).   [48]ἐντέλλω, *I command* (15). This verb only occurs in the middle voice in our literature (BAGD, s.v.). [49]ὅραμα, -ατος, τό, *vision* (12).   [50]Translate ἕως οὗ as *until* (BAGD, s.v., ἕως, II.1.b.α).   [51]See verse 14.

Reading 6 | Matthew 17:11–16

11. ὁ δὲ ἀποκριθεὶς εἶπεν, Ἡλίας[52] μὲν ἔρχεται καὶ ἀποκαταστήσει[53] πάντα· **12.** λέγω δὲ ὑμῖν ὅτι Ἡλίας ἤδη ἦλθεν, καὶ οὐκ ἐπέγνωσαν αὐτὸν ἀλλὰ ἐποίησαν ἐν αὐτῷ ὅσα <u>ἠθέλησαν</u>· οὕτως καὶ ὁ υἱὸς τοῦ ἀνθρώπου μέλλει πάσχειν ὑπ' αὐτῶν. **13.** τότε συνῆκαν[54] οἱ μαθηταὶ ὅτι περὶ Ἰωάννου τοῦ βαπτιστοῦ[55] εἶπεν αὐτοῖς.

14. Καὶ ἐλθόντων πρὸς τὸν ὄχλον προσῆλθεν αὐτῷ ἄνθρωπος γονυπετῶν[56] αὐτὸν **15.** καὶ λέγων, Κύριε, ἐλέησόν[57] μου τὸν υἱόν, ὅτι σεληνιάζεται[58] καὶ κακῶς πάσχει· πολλάκις[59] γὰρ πίπτει εἰς τὸ πῦρ καὶ πολλάκις εἰς τὸ ὕδωρ. **16.** καὶ <u>προσήνεγκα</u> αὐτὸν τοῖς μαθηταῖς σου, καὶ οὐκ ἠδυνήθησαν αὐτὸν <u>θεραπεῦσαι</u>.

Parsing: ἠθέλησαν _____

                προσήνεγκα _____

                θεραπεῦσαι _____

Translation: _____

---

[52]See verse 16:14.   [53]ἀποκαθίστημι, *I restore* (8).   [54]συνίημι, *I understand, comprehend* [Vocab. 9].
[55]See verse 16:14.   [56]γονυπετέω, *I fall upon my knees, kneel down* (4).   [57]ἐλεέω, *I have mercy, am merciful*
[Vocab. 7].   [58]σεληνιάζομαι, *I am a lunatic, am moon-struck* (2).   [59]πολλάκις, *often, many times* (18).

Vocabulary

Friends	Memory Aids
ἁμαρτάνω, *I sin, do wrong* (43).	ἁμαρτία—*sin.*
δεύτερος, -α, -ον, *second, secondly* (43).	Deutero—*second*, as in Deuteronomy
διέρχομαι, *I go through, cross over* (43).	I *go* (ἔρχομαι) *through* (διά).
ἐργάζομαι, *I work, do* (41).	ἔργον—*work.*
εὐλογέω, *I bless, speak well of* (42).	Eulogy—a speech in honor of a person.
Ἡρῴδης, -ου, ὁ, *Herod* (43).	Just like it sounds.
θεραπεύω, *I heal, serve* (43).	Therapy—used to *heal* the sick.
Ἰουδαία, -ας, ἡ, *Judea* (43).	Pronounce the Ἰ as an English *J.*
Ἰούδας, -α, ὁ, *Judas, Judah* (44).	Pronounce the Ἰ as an English *J.*
λύω, *I loose, untie* (42).	An old friend from *BBG.*
παρίστημι, *I place beside, stand by* (41).	I set (ἵστημι) *beside* (πάρα).
σπέρμα, -ατος, τό, *seed, descendants* (43).	Sperm—human *seed.*
φωνέω, *I call, call out* (43).	I use my voice (φωνή) to *call out.*
Cousins	
ἀνάστασις, -εως, ἡ, *resurrection, rise* (42).	Like ἀνίστημι—I raise, bring to life.
γενεά, -ᾶς, ἡ, *generation, family* (43).	I beget (γεννάω) a *family* (γενεά).
κατοικέω, *I inhabit, dwell* (44).	*I inhabit* a home (οἶκος).
πάντοτε, *always, at all times* (41).	Like πᾶς, πᾶσα, πᾶν—*all.*
πάσχω, *I suffer, die* (42).	The <u>pasch</u>al lamb *suffers* (πάσχω).
σεαυτοῦ, -ῆς, *of yourself* (43).	Second personal pronoun you (σε) plus αὐτός (self).
σήμερον, *today* (41).	Day (ἡμέρα) is hidden in this word.
Strangers	
ἄξιος, -α, -ον, *worthy, comparable* (41).	The holy one (ἅγιος) is *worthy* (ἄξιος).
δέω, *I bind, tie* (43).	I loose (λύω) and *bind* (δέω).
ἐγγίζω, *I come near, approach* (42).	I *approach* with an egg (ἐγγ).
θαυμάζω, *I marvel, wonder at* (43).	A <u>thauma</u>turge performs *marvels.*
Ἰάκωβος, -ου, ὁ, *James* (42).	Jacob (which this resembles) is Ἰακώβ.
καινός, -ή, -όν, *new, unused* (42).	It is <u>kind</u> of a *new* thing.
μέρος, -ους, τό, *part, piece* (42).	A computer has nu<u>merous</u> *parts.*
τέσσαρες, -α, *four* (41).	
τιμή, -ῆς, ἡ, *honor, price, value* (41).	It was a <u>time</u> for *honor.*
χωρίς, *separately, without, apart from* (41).	<u>Chorus</u> members do not sing *separately.*

Week Four

John 6:25–59

Reading 1 | John 6:25–29

25. καὶ εὑρόντες αὐτὸν πέραν¹ τῆς θαλάσσης εἶπον αὐτῷ, Ῥαββί, πότε² ὧδε γέγονας;

26. ἀπεκρίθη αὐτοῖς ὁ Ἰησοῦς καὶ εἶπεν, Ἀμὴν ἀμὴν λέγω ὑμῖν, ζητεῖτέ με οὐχ ὅτι εἴδετε σημεῖα ἀλλ᾽ ὅτι ἐφάγετε ἐκ τῶν ἄρτων καὶ ἐχορτάσθητε.³ **27.** ἐργάζεσθε μὴ τὴν βρῶσιν⁴ τὴν ἀπολλυμένην ἀλλὰ τὴν βρῶσιν τὴν μένουσαν εἰς ζωὴν αἰώνιον, ἣν ὁ υἱὸς τοῦ ἀνθρώπου ὑμῖν δώσει· τοῦτον γὰρ ὁ πατὴρ ἐσφράγισεν⁵ ὁ θεός.

28. εἶπον οὖν πρὸς αὐτόν, Τί ποιῶμεν ἵνα ἐργαζώμεθα τὰ ἔργα τοῦ θεου;

29. ἀπεκρίθη ὁ Ἰησοῦς καὶ εἶπεν αὐτοῖς, Τοῦτό ἐστιν τὸ ἔργον τοῦ θεοῦ, ἵνα πιστεύητε εἰς ὃν ἀπέστειλεν ἐκεῖνος.

Parsing: γέγονας   _____

               ἐφάγετε   _____

               μένουσαν _____

Translation: _____

_____

_____

_____

_____

_____

_____

_____

_____

_____

_____

_____

_____

---

¹πέραν, *on the other side, across* [Vocab. 10].   ²πότε, *when* (19).   ³χορτάζω, *I feed, fill* (16).
⁴βρῶσις, -εως, ἡ, *eating, food* (11).   ⁵σφραγίζω, *I put a seal on, mark* (15).

Reading 2 | John 6:30–35

30. εἶπον οὖν αὐτῷ, Τί οὖν ποιεῖς σὺ σημεῖον, ἵνα ἴδωμεν καὶ πιστεύσωμέν <u>σοι</u>; τί ἐργάζῃ; **31.** οἱ πατέρες ἡμῶν τὸ μάννα⁶ ἔφαγον ἐν τῇ ἐρήμῳ, καθώς ἐστιν γεγραμμένον, Ἄρτον ἐκ τοῦ οὐρανοῦ ἔδωκεν αὐτοῖς φαγεῖν.

32. εἶπεν οὖν αὐτοῖς ὁ Ἰησοῦς, Ἀμὴν ἀμὴν λέγω ὑμῖν, οὐ Μωϋσῆς <u>δέδωκεν</u> ὑμῖν τὸν ἄρτον ἐκ τοῦ οὐρανοῦ, ἀλλ᾽ ὁ πατήρ μου δίδωσιν ὑμῖν τὸν ἄρτον ἐκ τοῦ οὐρανοῦ τὸν ἀληθινόν·⁷ **33.** ὁ γὰρ ἄρτος τοῦ θεοῦ ἐστιν ὁ καταβαίνων ἐκ τοῦ οὐρανοῦ καὶ ζωὴν <u>διδοὺς</u> τῷ κόσμῳ.

34. Εἶπον οὖν πρὸς αὐτόν, Κύριε, πάντοτε δὸς ἡμῖν τὸν ἄρτον τοῦτον.

35. εἶπεν αὐτοῖς ὁ Ἰησοῦς, Ἐγώ εἰμι ὁ ἄρτος τῆς ζωῆς· ὁ ἐρχόμενος πρὸς ἐμὲ οὐ μὴ πεινάσῃ,⁸ καὶ ὁ πιστεύων εἰς ἐμὲ οὐ μὴ⁹ διψήσει¹⁰ πώποτε.¹¹

Parsing: σοι   _____

          δέδωκεν _____

          διδοὺς   _____

Translation: _____

_____

_____

_____

_____

_____

_____

_____

_____

_____

_____

_____

---

⁶μάννα, τό, *manna* (4).   ⁷ἀληθινός, -ή, -όν, *true, real* [Vocab. 7].   ⁸πεινάω, *I hunger, am hungry* [Vocab. 10].
⁹How can you reconcile the use of μή with a verb in the indicative mood (διψήσει)?   ¹⁰διψάω, *I thirst, long for* (16).
¹¹πώποτε, *ever, at any time* (6).

Reading 3 | John 6:36–40

36. ἀλλ᾽ εἶπον ὑμῖν ὅτι καὶ ἑωράκατέ με καὶ οὐ πιστεύετε. **37.** Πᾶν ὃ δίδωσίν μοι ὁ πατὴρ πρὸς ἐμὲ ἥξει,[12] καὶ τὸν ἐρχόμενον πρὸς ἐμὲ οὐ μὴ <u>ἐκβάλω</u> ἔξω, **38.** ὅτι καταβέβηκα ἀπὸ τοῦ οὐρανοῦ οὐχ ἵνα ποιῶ τὸ θέλημα τὸ ἐμὸν ἀλλὰ τὸ θέλημα τοῦ πέμψαντός με· **39.** τοῦτο δέ ἐστιν τὸ θέλημα τοῦ πέμψαντός με, ἵνα πᾶν ὃ δέδωκέν μοι μη ἀπολέσω ἐξ αὐτοῦ ἀλλὰ <u>ἀναστήσω</u> αὐτὸ ἐν τῇ ἐσχάτῃ ἡμέρᾳ. **40.** τοῦτο γὰρ ἐστιν τὸ θέλημα τοῦ πατρός μου, ἵνα πᾶς ὁ θεωρῶν τὸν υἱὸν καὶ πιστεύων εἰς αὐτὸν <u>ἔχῃ</u> ζωὴν αἰώνιον, καὶ ἀναστήσω αὐτὸν ἐγὼ ἐν τῇ ἐσχάτῃ ἡμέρᾳ.

Parsing: ἐκβάλω _____

ἀναστήσω _____

ἔχῃ _____

Translation: _____

_____

_____

_____

_____

_____

_____

_____

_____

_____

_____

_____

_____

_____

_____

_____

_____

---

[12] ἥκω, *I have come, am present* [Vocab. 8].

Reading 4	John 6:41–46

41. Ἐγόγγυζον[13] οὖν οἱ Ἰουδαῖοι περὶ αὐτοῦ ὅτι εἶπεν, Ἐγώ εἰμι ὁ ἄρτος ὁ <u>καταβὰς</u> ἐκ τοῦ οὐρανοῦ, **42.** καὶ ἔλεγον, Οὐχ οὗτός ἐστιν Ἰησοῦς ὁ υἱὸς Ἰωσήφ,[14] οὗ ἡμεῖς οἴδαμεν τὸν πατέρα καὶ τὴν μητέρα; πῶς νῦν λέγει ὅτι Ἐκ τοῦ οὐρανοῦ καταβέβηκα;

43. ἀπεκρίθη Ἰησοῦς καὶ εἶπεν αὐτοῖς, Μὴ γογγύζετε μετ᾽ ἀλλήλων. **44.** οὐδεὶς δύναται <u>ἐλθεῖν</u> πρός με ἐὰν μὴ ὁ πατὴρ ὁ πέμψας με ἑλκύσῃ[15] αὐτόν, κἀγὼ ἀναστήσω αὐτὸν ἐν τῇ ἐσχάτῃ ἡμέρᾳ. **45.** ἔστιν <u>γεγραμμένον</u> ἐν τοῖς προφήταις, Καὶ ἔσονται πάντες διδακτοὶ[16] θεοῦ· πᾶς ὁ ἀκούσας παρὰ τοῦ πατρὸς καὶ μαθὼν[17] ἔρχεται πρὸς ἐμέ. **46.** οὐχ ὅτι τὸν πατέρα ἑώρακέν τις εἰ μὴ ὁ ὢν παρὰ τοῦ θεοῦ, οὗτος ἑώρακεν τὸν πατέρα.

Parsing: καταβὰς   _____

ἐλθεῖν   _____

γεγραμμένον   _____

Translation: _____

_____

_____

_____

_____

_____

_____

_____

_____

_____

_____

_____

_____

---

[13]γογγύζω, *I grumble, mutter* (8).   [14]Ἰωσήφ, ὁ, *Joseph* [Vocab. 5].   [15]ἕλκω, *I drag, draw* (8).   [16]διδακτός, -ή, -όν, *instructed, taught* (3).   [17]μανθάνω, *I learn, find out* [Vocab. 9].

Reading 5 | John 6:47–53

47. ἀμὴν ἀμὴν λέγω ὑμῖν, ὁ πιστεύων ἔχει ζωὴν αἰώνιον. **48.** ἐγώ εἰμι ὁ ἄρτος τῆς ζωῆς.
49. οἱ πατέρες ὑμῶν ἔφαγον ἐν τῇ ἐρήμῳ τὸ μάννα καὶ <u>ἀπέθανον</u>· **50.** οὗτός ἐστιν ὁ ἄρτος ὁ ἐκ
τοῦ οὐρανοῦ καταβαίνων ἵνα τις ἐξ αὐτοῦ <u>φάγῃ</u> καὶ μὴ ἀποθάνῃ. **51.** ἐγώ εἰμι ὁ ἄρτος ὁ ζῶν
ὁ ἐκ τοῦ οὐρανοῦ καταβάς· ἐάν τις φάγῃ ἐκ τούτου τοῦ ἄρτου ζήσει εἰς τὸν αἰῶνα· καὶ ὁ
ἄρτος δὲ ὃν ἐγὼ δώσω ἡ σάρξ μού ἐστιν ὑπὲρ τῆς τοῦ κόσμου ζωῆς.

52. Ἐμάχοντο[18] οὖν πρὸς ἀλλήλους οἱ Ἰουδαῖοι λέγοντες, Πῶς δύναται οὗτος ἡμῖν
<u>δοῦναι</u> τὴν σάρκα [αὐτοῦ] φαγεῖν;

53. εἶπεν οὖν αὐτοῖς ὁ Ἰησοῦς, Ἀμὴν ἀμὴν λέγω ὑμῖν, ἐὰν μὴ φάγητε τὴν σάρκα τοῦ
υἱοῦ τοῦ ἀνθρώπου καὶ πίητε αὐτοῦ τὸ αἷμα, οὐκ ἔχετε ζωὴν ἐν ἑαυτοῖς.

Parsing: ἀπέθανον _____

φάγῃ _____

δοῦναι _____

Translation: _____

_____

_____

_____

_____

_____

_____

_____

_____

_____

_____

_____

_____

_____

---

[18]μάχομαι, _I fight, quarrel_ (4).

> **Reading 6** | **John 6:54–59**

54. ὁ τρώγων[19] μου τὴν σάρκα καὶ <u>πίνων</u> μου τὸ αἷμα ἔχει ζωὴν αἰώνιον, κἀγὼ ἀναστήσω αὐτὸν τῇ ἐσχάτῃ ἡμέρᾳ· **55.** ἡ γὰρ σάρξ μου ἀληθής[20] ἐστιν βρῶσις,[21] καὶ τὸ αἷμά μου ἀληθής ἐστιν πόσις.[22] **56.** ὁ τρώγων μου τὴν σάρκα καὶ πίνων μου τὸ αἷμα ἐν ἐμοὶ μένει κἀγὼ ἐν αὐτῷ. **57.** καθὼς ἀπέστειλέν με ὁ ζῶν πατὴρ κἀγὼ <u>ζῶ</u> διὰ τὸν πατέρα, καὶ ὁ τρώγων με κἀκεῖνος[23] ζήσει δι᾽ ἐμέ. **58.** οὗτός ἐστιν ὁ ἄρτος ὁ ἐξ <u>οὐρανοῦ</u> καταβάς, οὐ καθὼς ἔφαγον οἱ πατέρες καὶ ἀπέθανον· ὁ τρώγων τοῦτον τὸν ἄρτον ζήσει εἰς τὸν αἰῶνα. **59.** Ταῦτα εἶπεν ἐν συναγωγῇ διδάσκων ἐν Καφαρναούμ.[24]

Parsing: πίνων

ζῶ

οὐρανοῦ

Translation:

---

[19]τρώγω, *I eat* (6). [20]ἀληθής, -ές, *true, righteous* [Vocab. 8]. [21]See verse 27. [22]πόσις, -εως, ἡ, *drinking, drink* (3). [23]κἀκεῖνος, -η, -ο, *and that one, even that one* (a contraction of καί and ἐκεῖνος) [Vocab. 11]. [24]Καφαρναούμ, ἡ, *Capernaum* (16).

Vocabulary

Friends	Memory Aids
διάβολος, -ον, *adj: slanderous; subst: the devil* (37).	Spanish: Diabolos—devil.
δικαιόω, *I justify, vindicate* (39).	δίκαιος—righteous.
ἐμαυτοῦ, -ῆς, *of myself* (37).	ἐμος (mine) plus αὐτός (self); cf. σεαυτοῦ
ἐπιτίθημι, *I lay upon, put upon* (39).	I put (τίθημι) *upon* (ἐπί).
καλῶς, *well, beautifully* (37).	καλός—beautiful.
Cousins	
ἄρχων, -οντος, ὁ, *ruler, lord* (37).	Archbishop—*ruler* of bishops.
διακονέω, *I serve, wait upon* (37).	Deacon—someone who *serves* the church.
ἐκεῖθεν, *from there, thence* (37).	ἐκεῖ—*there*.
εὐχαριστέω, *I give thanks* (38).	Eucharist—a thanksgiving feast.
μισέω, *I hate, detest* (40).	Misogynist—someone who *hates* women.
μνημεῖον, -ου, τό, *tomb, monument* (40).	Mnemonics and *monuments* aid the memory.
ὀλίγος, -η, -ον, *small, little, short* (40).	Oligarchy—a state ruled by a *small* number of people.
οἰκοδομέω, *I build, edify* (40).	*I build* a home (οἰκία).
πέντε, *five* (38).	Pentagram—*five*-sided object.
τέλος, -ους, τό, *end, goal, tax* (40).	Telephone—A voice (φωνή) at the *end* of the line.
Strangers	
ἅπτομαι, ἅπτω, *I touch, kindle* (39).	A *touch* is apt to *kindle* a fire.
βούλομαι, *I wish, desire* (37).	
ἐπιθυμία, -ας, ἡ, *desire, lust* (38).	
ἑτοιμάζω, *I prepare, put or keep in readiness* (40).	*I prepare* to make matzoh balls.
θύρα, -ας, ἡ, *door, gate* (39).	I walk through–a θύρα.
ἱκανός, -ή, -όν, *sufficient, able* (39).	I can, because I am *sufficient*.
καυχάομαι, *I boast, pride myself* (37).	Because I am cocky, *I boast*.
κλαίω, *I weep, cry* (40).	Don't κλαίω (*cry*) for me, Argentina.
λογίζομαι, *I calculate, count* (40).	I use logic to λογίζομαι (*calculate*).
πειράζω, *I try, test, attempt* (38).	Peirastic—*attempting* an experiment.
περισσεύω, *I abound, am left over* (39).	Perissosyllabic—a *left over* syllable.
πλανάω, *I lead astray, deceive* (39).	I plan to *deceive* you.
πράσσω, *I do, practice* (39).	*Practice*, praxis, πράσσω.
πρόβατον, -ου, τό, *sheep* (39).	The *sheep* are on probation.
ὑποτάσσω, *I subject, subordinate* (38).	

Week Five

John 12:44–13:30

Reading 1	John 12:44–50

44. Ἰησοῦς δὲ ἔκραξεν καὶ εἶπεν, Ὁ πιστεύων εἰς ἐμὲ οὐ πιστεύει εἰς ἐμὲ ἀλλὰ εἰς τὸν πέμψαντά με, **45.** καὶ ὁ θεωρῶν ἐμὲ θεωρεῖ τὸν πέμψαντα με. **46.** ἐγὼ φῶς εἰς τὸν κόσμον ἐλήλυθα, ἵνα πᾶς ὁ πιστεύων εἰς ἐμὲ ἐν τῇ σκοτίᾳ[1] μὴ μείνη.

47. καὶ ἐάν τίς μου ἀκούσῃ τῶν ῥημάτων καὶ μὴ φυλάξῃ,[2] ἐγὼ οὐ κρίνω αὐτόν, οὐ γὰρ ἦλθον ἵνα κρίνω τὸν κόσμον ἀλλ᾽ ἵνα σώσω τὸν κόσμον. **48.** ὁ ἀθετῶν[3] ἐμὲ καὶ μὴ λαμβάνων τὰ ῥήματά μου ἔχει τὸν κρίνοντα αὐτόν· ὁ λόγος ὃν ἐλάλησα ἐκεῖνος κρινεῖ αὐτὸν ἐν τῇ ἐσχάτῃ ἡμέρᾳ· **49.** ὅτι ἐγὼ ἐξ ἐμαυτοῦ οὐκ ἐλάλησα, ἀλλ᾽ ὁ πέμψας με πατὴρ αὐτός μοι ἐντολὴν δέδωκεν τί εἴπω καὶ τί λαλήσω. **50.** καὶ οἶδα ὅτι ἡ ἐντολὴ αὐτοῦ ζωὴ αἰώνιός ἐστιν. ἃ οὖν ἐγὼ λαλῶ, καθὼς εἴρηκέν μοι ὁ πατήρ, οὕτως λαλῶ.

Parsing: ἐλήλυθα   _____

             μείνη   _____

             κρίνοντα   _____

Translation: _____

_____

_____

_____

_____

_____

_____

_____

_____

_____

---

[1] σκοτία, -ας, ἡ, *darkness, gloom* (16).   [2] φυλάσσω, *I keep, guard, watch* [Vocab. 6].   [3] ἀθετέω, *I declare invalid, nullify, set aside* (16).

Reading 2 | John 13:1–6

1. Πρὸ δὲ τῆς ἑορτῆς[4] τοῦ πάσχα[5] <u>εἰδὼς</u> ὁ Ἰησοῦς ὅτι ἦλθεν αὐτοῦ ἡ ὥρα ἵνα μεταβῇ[6] ἐκ τοῦ κόσμου τούτου πρὸς τὸν πατέρα, ἀγαπήσας τοὺς ἰδίους τοὺς ἐν τῷ κόσμῳ, εἰς τέλος ἠγάπησεν αὐτούς.

2. καὶ δείπνου[7] γινομένου, τοῦ διαβόλου ἤδη <u>βεβληκότος</u> εἰς τὴν καρδίαν ἵνα <u>παραδοῖ</u> αὐτὸν Ἰούδας Σίμωνος Ἰσκαριώτου,[8] **3.** εἰδὼς ὅτι πάντα ἔδωκεν αὐτῷ ὁ πατὴρ εἰς τὰς χεῖρας καὶ ὅτι ἀπὸ θεοῦ ἐξῆλθεν καὶ πρὸς τὸν θεὸν ὑπάγει, **4.** ἐγείρεται ἐκ τοῦ δείπνου καὶ τίθησιν τὰ ἱμάτια, καὶ λαβὼν λέντιον[9] διέζωσεν[10] ἑαυτόν. **5.** εἶτα[11] βάλλει ὕδωρ εἰς τὸν νιπτῆρα[12] καὶ ἤρξατο νίπτειν[13] τοὺς πόδας τῶν μαθητῶν καὶ ἐκμάσσειν[14] τῷ λεντίῳ ᾧ ἦν διεζωσμένος.

6. ἔρχεται οὖν πρὸς Σίμωνα Πέτρον. λέγει αὐτῷ, Κύριε, σύ μου νίπτεις τοὺς πόδας;

Parsing: εἰδὼς   _____

              βεβληκότος _____

              παραδοῖ   _____

Translation: _____

---

[4]ἑορτή, -ῆς, ἡ, *festival, feast* [Vocab. 9].   [5]πάσχα, τό, *Passover, Passover meal* [Vocab. 7].   [6]μεταβαίνω, *I go or pass over, move* (12).   [7]δεῖπνον, -ου, τό, *dinner, supper* (16).   [8]Ἰσκαριώτης, -ου, ὁ, *Iscariot* (8). [9]λέντιον, -ου, τό, *towel* (2).   [10]διαζώννυμι, *I tie around* (3).   [11]εἶτα, *then, next* (15).   [12]νιπτήρ, -ῆρος, ὁ, *washbasin* (1).   [13]νίπτω, *I wash* (18).   [14]ἐκμάσσω, *I wipe dry* (5).

Reading 3 | John 13:7–11

7. ἀπεκρίθη Ἰησοῦς καὶ εἶπεν αὐτῷ, Ὃ ἐγὼ ποιῶ σὺ οὐκ οἶδας ἄρτι, <u>γνώσῃ</u> δὲ μετὰ ταῦτα.

8. λέγει αὐτῷ Πέτρος, Οὐ μὴ νίψῃς[15] μου τοὺς πόδας εἰς τὸν αἰῶνα. ἀπεκρίθη Ἰησοῦς αὐτῷ, Ἐὰν μὴ νίψω σε, οὐκ ἔχεις μέρος μετ' <u>ἐμοῦ</u>.

9. λέγει αὐτῷ Σίμων Πέτρος, Κύριε, μὴ τοὺς πόδας μου μόνον ἀλλὰ καὶ τὰς χεῖρας καὶ τὴν κεφαλήν.

10. λέγει αὐτῷ ὁ Ἰησοῦς, Ὁ λελουμένος[16] οὐκ ἔχει χρείαν εἰ μὴ τοὺς πόδας νίψασθαι, ἀλλ' ἔστιν καθαρὸς[17] ὅλος· καὶ ὑμεῖς καθαροί ἐστε, ἀλλ' οὐχὶ πάντες. **11.** ᾔδει[18] γὰρ τὸν <u>παραδιδόντα</u> αὐτόν· διὰ τοῦτο εἶπεν ὅτι Οὐχὶ πάντες καθαροί ἐστε.

Parsing: γνώσῃ

ἐμοῦ

παραδιδόντα

Translation:

---

[15]See verse 5.   [16]λούω, *I wash, bathe* (5).   [17]καθαρός, -ά, -όν, *clean, pure* [Vocab. 8].   [18]This is the pluperfect form of οἶδα. Translate it as *he knew* (see *BBG*, 232; Wallace, 586).

Reading 4 | **John 13:12–18**

12. Ὅτε οὖν ἔνιψεν[19] τοὺς πόδας αὐτῶν ἔλαβεν τὰ ἱμάτια αὐτοῦ καὶ ἀνέπεσεν[20] πάλιν, εἶπεν αὐτοῖς, Γινώσκετε τί <u>πεποίηκα</u> ὑμῖν; **13.** ὑμεῖς φωνεῖτέ με Ὁ διδάσκαλος καὶ Ὁ κύριος, καὶ καλῶς λέγετε, εἰμὶ γάρ. **14.** εἰ οὖν ἐγὼ ἔνιψα ὑμῶν τοὺς πόδας ὁ κύριος καὶ ὁ διδάσκαλος, καὶ ὑμεῖς ὀφείλετε ἀλλήλων νίπτειν τοὺς πόδας· **15.** ὑπόδειγμα[21] γὰρ <u>ἔδωκα</u> ὑμῖν ἵνα καθὼς ἐγὼ ἐποίησα ὑμῖν καὶ ὑμεῖς ποιῆτε. **16.** ἀμὴν ἀμὴν λέγω ὑμῖν, οὐκ ἔστιν δοῦλος μείζων τοῦ κυρίου αὐτοῦ οὐδὲ ἀπόστολος μείζων τοῦ πέμψαντος αὐτόν. **17.** εἰ ταῦτα οἴδατε, <u>μακάριοί</u> ἐστε ἐὰν ποιῆτε αὐτά.

18. οὐ περὶ πάντων ὑμῶν λέγω· ἐγὼ οἶδα τίνας ἐξελεξάμην·[22] ἀλλ᾽ ἵνα ἡ γραφὴ πληρωθῇ, Ὁ τρώγων[23] μου τὸν ἄρτον ἐπῆρεν[24] ἐπ᾽ ἐμὲ τὴν πτέρναν[25] αὐτοῦ.

Parsing: πεποίηκα _____

    ἔδωκα _____

    μακάριοι _____

Translation: _____

_____

_____

_____

_____

_____

_____

_____

_____

_____

_____

_____

---

[19]See verse 5.   [20]ἀναπίπτω, *I lie down, recline* (12).   [21]ὑπόδειγμα, -ατος, τό, *example, model* (6).
[22]ἐκλέγομαι, *I choose* [Vocab. 11].   [23]τρώγω, *I eat* (6).   [24]ἐπαίρω, *I lift up, am in opposition* (19).
[25]πτέρνα, -ης, ἡ, *heel* (1).

Reading 5 | John 13:19–25

19. ἀπ᾽ ἄρτι λέγω ὑμῖν πρὸ τοῦ γενέσθαι,[26] ἵνα πιστεύσητε ὅταν γένηται ὅτι ἐγώ εἰμι.

20. ἀμὴν ἀμὴν λέγω ὑμῖν, ὁ λαμβάνων ἄν τινα <u>πέμψω</u> ἐμὲ λαμβάνει, ὁ δὲ ἐμὲ λαμβάνων λαμβάνει τὸν πέμψαντά με.

21. Ταῦτα εἰπὼν [ὁ] Ἰησοῦς ἐταράχθη[27] τῷ πνεύματι καὶ <u>ἐμαρτύρησεν</u> καὶ εἶπεν, Ἀμὴν ἀμὴν λέγω ὑμῖν ὅτι εἷς ἐξ ὑμῶν παραδώσει με.

22. ἔβλεπον εἰς ἀλλήλους οἱ μαθηταὶ ἀπορούμενοι[28] περὶ τίνος λέγει. **23.** ἦν ἀνακείμενος[29] εἷς ἐκ τῶν μαθητῶν αὐτοῦ ἐν τῷ κόλπῳ[30] τοῦ Ἰησοῦ, ὃν <u>ἠγάπα</u> ὁ Ἰησοῦς· **24.** νεύει[31] οὖν τούτῳ Σίμων Πέτρος πυθέσθαι[32] τίς ἂν εἴη[33] περὶ οὗ λέγει.

25. ἀναπεσὼν[34] οὖν ἐκεῖνος οὕτως ἐπὶ τὸ στῆθος[35] τοῦ Ἰησοῦ λέγει αὐτῷ, Κύριε, τίς ἐστιν;

Parsing: πέμψω _____

ἐμαρτύρησεν _____

ἠγάπα _____

Translation: _____

_____

_____

_____

_____

_____

_____

_____

_____

_____

_____

_____

_____

_____

---

[26]πρό + infinitive can be translated as *before* (see *BBG*, 297). [27]ταράσσω, *I stir up, disturb* (17). [28]ἀπορέω, *I am at a loss, uncertain* (6). [29]ἀνάκειμαι, *I lie, recline* (14). [30]κόλπος, -ου, ὁ, *chest, breast, bosom* (6). [31]νεύω, *I motion, nod* (2). [32]πυνθάνομαι, *I inquire, ask, learn* (12). [33]This is the optative mood of εἰμί. Translate it as *it might be* (see *BBG*, 325–326). [34]See verse 12. [35]στῆθος, -ους, τό, *chest, breast* (5).

Reading 6 | John 13:26–30

26. ἀποκρίνεται ὁ Ἰησοῦς, Ἐκεῖνός ἐστιν ᾧ ἐγὼ βάψω[36] τὸ ψωμίον[37] καὶ δώσω αὐτῷ.

βάψας οὖν τὸ ψωμίον δίδωσιν Ἰούδᾳ Σίμωνος Ἰσκαριώτου.[38] **27.** καὶ μετὰ τὸ ψωμίον τότε

εἰσῆλθεν εἰς ἐκεῖνον ὁ Σατανᾶς. λέγει οὖν αὐτῷ ὁ Ἰησοῦς, Ὃ ποιεῖς <u>ποίησον</u> τάχιον.[39]

28. τοῦτο δὲ οὐδεὶς <u>ἔγνω</u> τῶν ἀνακειμένων[40] πρὸς τί εἶπεν αὐτῷ· **29.** τινὲς γὰρ ἐδόκουν, ἐπεὶ[41]

τὸ γλωσσόκομον[42] <u>εἶχεν</u> Ἰούδας, ὅτι λέγει αὐτῷ ὁ Ἰησοῦς, Ἀγόρασον[43] ὧν χρείαν ἔχομεν εἰς

τὴν ἑορτήν, ἢ τοῖς πτωχοῖς ἵνα τι δῷ. **30.** λαβὼν οὖν τὸ ψωμίον ἐκεῖνος ἐξῆλθεν εὐθύς· ἦν δὲ

νύξ.

Parsing: ποίησον _____

ἔγνω _____

εἶχεν _____

Translation: _____

_____

_____

_____

_____

_____

_____

_____

_____

_____

_____

_____

_____

_____

[36]βάπτω, *I dip* (4).   [37]ψωμίον, -ου, τό, *piece of bread* (4).   [38]See verse 2.   [39]τάχιον, *quickly* (5).
[40]See verse 23.   [41]ἐπεί, *because* [Vocab. 8].   [42]γλωσσόκομον, -ου, τό, *money box* (2).   [43]ἀγοράζω, *I buy,*
purchase [Vocab. 6].

Vocabulary

Friends	Memory Aids
ἅπας, -ασα, -αν, *all, whole* (34).	πᾶς—each, every, *all.*
βιβλίον, -ου, τό, *book, scroll* (34).	Bible—a holy *book.*
βλασφημέω, *I blaspheme, revile* (34).	*Blaspheme.*
διακονία, -ας, ἡ, *service, ministry, deacon* (34).	*Deacon.*
Ἰωσήφ, ὁ, *Joseph* (35).	Pronounce the *I* as an English *J.*
μαρτυρία, -ας, ἡ, *testimony, witness* (37).	μαρτυρέω—I bear *witness.*
μάρτυς, -υρος, ὁ, *witness, martyr* (35).	μαρτυρέω—I bear *witness.*
μήτε, *and not, neither, nor* (34).	*And* (τέ) *not* (μή).
παραγίνομαι, *I come, arrive* (37).	I *come* (γίνομαι) from (παρά).
προσευχή, -ῆς, ἡ, *prayer, place of prayer* (36).	προσεύχομαι—I pray.
Σατανᾶς, -ᾶ, ὁ, *Satan, the Adversary* (36).	Just like it sounds.
Φίλιππος, -ου, ὁ, *Philip* (36).	Just like it sounds.
ὥσπερ, *as, just as* (36).	Like ὡς—*as.*
Cousins	
ἀγρός, -οῦ, ὁ, *field, country* (36).	Agriculture requires a *field.*
μετανοέω, *I repent, change my mind* (34).	Metanoia—repentance.
οἶνος, -ου, ὁ, *wine, vineyard* (34).	Change the "o" into a "w."
Strangers	
ἀρνέομαι, *I refuse, deny* (33).	
ἄρτι, *now, just* (36).	Art *just now* is in terrible shape.
ἀσθενέω, *I am weak, powerless* (33).	Asthmatics have *weak* lungs.
δείκνυμι, *I show, explain* (33).	Apodeictic—clearly *shown.*
στρέφω, *I turn, change, return* (21).	Strep germs *turn* me sick.
ἐπιστρέφω, *I turn, return* (36).	στρέφω—*I turn.*
ὑποστρέφω, *I turn back, return* (35).	στρέφω—*I turn.*
εὐθέως, *immediately, at once* (36).	Euthanasia is an *immediate* death.
μέλος, -ους, τό, *member, part* (34).	I had *part* of a melon.
ὀπίσω, *behind, after* (35).	
ὀργή, -ῆς, ἡ, *anger, wrath* (36).	I played the organ in *anger.*
οὖς, ὠτός, τό, *ear, hearing* (36).	Otitis—inflammation of the *ear.*
ὀφείλω, *I owe, ought* (35).	
περιτομή, -ῆς, ἡ, *circumcision, the circumcised* (36).	Cutting (τομή) around (περί).
πτωχός, -ή, -όν, *poor, poor person* (34).	Sometimes, the *poor* get ptomaine poisoning.

Week Six

John 13:31–14:31

Reading 1 | John 13:31–35

31. Ὅτε οὖν ἐξῆλθεν λέγει Ἰησοῦς, Νῦν <u>ἐδοξάσθη</u> ὁ υἱὸς τοῦ ἀνθρώπου, καὶ ὁ θεὸς ἐδοξάσθη ἐν αὐτῷ· **32.** εἰ ὁ θεὸς ἐδοξάσθη ἐν αὐτῷ, καὶ ὁ θεὸς <u>δοξάσει</u> αὐτὸν ἐν αὐτῷ, καὶ εὐθὺς δοξάσει αὐτόν.

33. τεκνία, ἔτι μικρὸν μεθ᾽ ὑμῶν εἰμι· ζητήσετέ με, καὶ καθὼς εἶπον τοῖς <u>Ἰουδαίοις</u> ὅτι Ὅπου ἐγὼ ὑπάγω ὑμεῖς οὐ δύνασθε ἐλθεῖν, καὶ ὑμῖν λέγω ἄρτι.

34. ἐντολὴν καινὴν δίδωμι ὑμῖν, ἵνα ἀγαπᾶτε ἀλλήλους, καθὼς ἠγάπησα ὑμᾶς ἵνα καὶ ὑμεῖς ἀγαπᾶτε ἀλλήλους. **35.** ἐν τούτῳ γνώσονται πάντες ὅτι ἐμοὶ μαθηταί ἐστε, ἐὰν ἀγάπην ἔχητε ἐν ἀλλήλοις.

Parsing: ἐδοξάσθη   _____

δοξάσει   _____

Ἰουδαίοις   _____

Translation: _____

_____

_____

_____

_____

_____

_____

_____

_____

_____

_____

_____

_____

Reading 2	John 13:36–14:4

36. Λέγει αὐτῷ Σίμων Πέτρος, Κύριε, ποῦ ὑπάγεις; ἀπεκρίθη Ἰησοῦς, Ὅπου ὑπάγω οὐ δύνασαί μοι νῦν ἀκολουθῆσαι, <u>ἀκολουθήσεις</u> δὲ ὕστερον.[1]

37. λέγει αὐτῷ ὁ Πέτρος, Κύριε, διὰ τί[2] οὐ δύναμαί σοι ἀκολουθῆσαι ἄρτι; τὴν ψυχήν μου ὑπὲρ σοῦ <u>θήσω</u>.

38. ἀποκρίνεται Ἰησοῦς, Τὴν ψυχήν σου ὑπὲρ ἐμοῦ θήσεις; ἀμὴν ἀμὴν λέγω σοι, οὐ μὴ ἀλέκτωρ[3] <u>φωνήσῃ</u> ἕως οὗ ἀρνήσῃ με τρίς.

14:1. Μὴ ταρασσέσθω[4] ὑμῶν ἡ καρδία· πιστεύετε εἰς τὸν θεόν, καὶ εἰς ἐμὲ πιστεύετε. **2.** ἐν τῇ οἰκίᾳ τοῦ πατρός μου μοναὶ[5] πολλαί εἰσιν· εἰ δὲ μή, εἶπον ἂν ὑμῖν ὅτι πορεύομαι ἑτοιμάσαι τόπον ὑμῖν; **3.** καὶ ἐὰν πορευθῶ καὶ ἑτοιμάσω τόπον ὑμῖν, πάλιν ἔρχομαι καὶ παραλήμψομαι ὑμᾶς πρὸς ἐμαυτόν, ἵνα ὅπου εἰμὶ ἐγὼ καὶ ὑμεῖς ἦτε. **4.** καὶ ὅπου ἐγὼ ὑπάγω οἴδατε τὴν ὁδόν.

Parsing: ἀκολουθήσεις _____

              θήσω _____

              φωνήσῃ _____

Translation: _____

_____

_____

_____

_____

_____

_____

_____

_____

_____

_____

_____

_____

_____

_____

_____

_____

---

[1] ὕστερος, α, ον, *later, latter, last* (12).   [2] διὰ τί literally, *on account of what*; can be translated *why* (BAGD, s.v. διά, B.II.2).   [3] ἀλέκτωρ, -ορος, ὁ, *rooster* (12).   [4] ταράσσω, *I disturb, trouble* (17).   [5] μονή, -ῆς, ἡ, *room, abode* (2).

Reading 3 | John 14:5–10

5. Λέγει αὐτῷ Θωμᾶς, Κύριε, οὐκ οἴδαμεν ποῦ ὑπάγεις· πῶς δυνάμεθα τὴν ὁδὸν <u>εἰδέναι</u>;

6. λέγει αὐτῷ ὁ Ἰησοῦς, Ἐγώ εἰμι ἡ ὁδὸς καὶ ἡ ἀλήθεια καὶ ἡ ζωή· οὐδεὶς ἔρχεται πρὸς τὸν πατέρα εἰ μὴ δι᾽ ἐμοῦ. **7.** εἰ ἐγνώκατέ με, καὶ τὸν πατέρα μου γνώσεσθε· καὶ ἀπ᾽ ἄρτι γινώσκετε αὐτὸν καὶ ἑωράκατε αὐτόν.

8. λέγει αὐτῷ Φίλιππος, Κύριε, <u>δεῖξον</u> ἡμῖν τὸν πατέρα, καὶ ἀρκεῖ⁶ ἡμῖν.

9. λέγει αὐτῷ ὁ Ἰησοῦς, Τοσούτῳ⁷ χρόνῳ μεθ᾽ ὑμῶν εἰμι καὶ οὐκ ἔγνωκάς με, Φίλιππε; ὁ <u>ἑωρακὼς</u> ἐμὲ ἑώρακεν τὸν πατέρα· πῶς σὺ λέγεις, Δεῖξον ἡμῖν τὸν πατέρα; **10.** οὐ πιστεύεις ὅτι ἐγὼ ἐν τῷ πατρὶ καὶ ὁ πατὴρ ἐν ἐμοί ἐστιν; τὰ ῥήματα ἃ ἐγὼ λέγω ὑμῖν ἀπ᾽ ἐμαυτοῦ οὐ λαλῶ· ὁ δὲ πατὴρ ἐν ἐμοὶ μένων ποιεῖ τὰ ἔργα αὐτοῦ.

Parsing: εἰδέναι _____

  δεῖξον _____

  ἑωρακὼς _____

Translation: _____

_____

_____

_____

_____

_____

_____

_____

_____

_____

_____

_____

---

⁶ἀρκέω, _I am satisfied, sufficient_ (8).   ⁷τοσοῦτος, -αύτη, -οῦτον, _so great, so much_ [Vocab 12].

Reading 4 | John 14:11–17

11. πιστεύετέ μοι ὅτι ἐγὼ ἐν τῷ πατρὶ καὶ ὁ πατὴρ ἐν ἐμοί· εἰ δὲ μή, διὰ τὰ ἔργα αὐτὰ πιστεύετε. **12.** ἀμὴν ἀμὴν λέγω ὑμῖν, ὁ πιστεύων εἰς ἐμὲ τὰ ἔργα ὰ ἐγὼ ποιῶ κἀκεῖνος[8] ποιήσει καὶ μείζονα τούτων ποιήσει, ὅτι ἐγὼ πρὸς τὸν πατέρα πορεύομαι· **13.** καὶ ὅ τι ἂν αἰτήσητε ἐν τῷ ὀνόματί μου τοῦτο ποιήσω, ἵνα δοξασθῇ ὁ πατὴρ ἐν τῷ υἱῷ· **14.** ἐάν τι αἰτήσητέ με ἐν τῷ ὀνόματί μου ἐγὼ ποιήσω.

15. Ἐὰν ἀγαπᾶτέ με, τὰς ἐντολὰς τὰς ἐμὰς τηρήσετε· **16.** κἀγὼ ἐρωτήσω τὸν πατέρα καὶ ἄλλον παράκλητον[9] δώσει ὑμῖν ἵνα μεθ᾽ ὑμῶν εἰς τὸν αἰῶνα ᾖ, **17.** τὸ πνεῦμα τῆς ἀληθείας, ὃ ὁ κόσμος οὐ δύναται λαβεῖν, ὅτι οὐ θεωρεῖ αὐτὸ οὐδὲ γινώσκει· ὑμεῖς γινώσκετε αὐτό, ὅτι παρ᾽ ὑμῖν μένει καὶ ἐν ὑμῖν ἔσται.

Parsing: ἃ   _____

            αἰτήσητέ   _____

            θεωρεῖ   _____

Translation: _____

_____

_____

_____

_____

_____

_____

_____

_____

_____

_____

_____

_____

_____

[8]κἀκεῖνος, -η, -ο, *and that one, also that one* [Vocab. 11].   [9]παράκλητος, -ου, ὁ, *advocate, helper, intercessor* (5).

Reading 5 | John 14:18–24

18. Οὐκ ἀφήσω ὑμᾶς ὀρφανούς,[10] ἔρχομαι πρὸς ὑμᾶς. **19.** ἔτι μικρὸν καὶ ὁ κόσμος με οὐκέτι θεωρεῖ, ὑμεῖς δὲ θεωρεῖτέ με, ὅτι ἐγὼ <u>ζῶ</u> καὶ ὑμεῖς ζήσετε. **20.** ἐν ἐκείνῃ τῇ ἡμέρᾳ γνώσεσθε ὑμεῖς ὅτι ἐγὼ ἐν τῷ πατρί μου καὶ ὑμεῖς ἐν ἐμοὶ κἀγὼ ἐν ὑμῖν. **21.** ὁ ἔχων τὰς ἐντολάς μου καὶ τηρῶν αὐτὰς ἐκεῖνός ἐστιν ὁ ἀγαπῶν με· ὁ δὲ ἀγαπῶν με <u>ἀγαπηθήσεται</u> ὑπὸ τοῦ πατρός μου, κἀγὼ ἀγαπήσω αὐτὸν καὶ ἐμφανίσω[11] αὐτῷ ἐμαυτόν.

22. Λέγει αὐτῷ Ἰούδας, οὐχ ὁ Ἰσκαριώτης,[12] Κύριε, καὶ τί γέγονεν ὅτι ἡμῖν μέλλεις ἐμφανίζειν σεαυτὸν καὶ οὐχὶ τῷ κόσμῳ;

23. ἀπεκρίθη Ἰησοῦς καὶ εἶπεν αὐτῷ, Ἐάν τις ἀγαπᾷ με τὸν λόγον μου τηρήσει, καὶ ὁ πατήρ μου ἀγαπήσει αὐτόν καὶ πρὸς αὐτὸν <u>ἐλευσόμεθα</u> καὶ μονὴν παρ᾽ αὐτῷ ποιησόμεθα. **24.** ὁ μὴ ἀγαπῶν με τοὺς λόγους μου οὐ τηρεῖ· καὶ ὁ λόγος ὃν ἀκούετε οὐκ ἔστιν ἐμὸς ἀλλὰ τοῦ πέμψαντός με πατρός.

Parsing: ζῶ _____

                 ἀγαπηθήσεται _____

                 ἐλευσόμεθα _____

Translation:

_____

_____

_____

_____

_____

_____

_____

_____

_____

_____

_____

---

[10]ὀρφανός, -ή, -όν, *orphaned* (used as a subst., *orphan*) (2).   [11]ἐμφανίζω, *I reveal, make visible* (10).
[12]Ἰσκαριώτης, -ου, ὁ, *Iscariot* (8).

Reading 6 | John 14:25–31

25. Ταῦτα λελάληκα ὑμῖν παρ᾽ ὑμῖν μένων· **26.** ὁ δὲ παράκλητος,[13] τὸ πνεῦμα τὸ ἅγιον ὃ πέμψει ὁ πατὴρ ἐν τῷ ὀνόματί μου, ἐκεῖνος ὑμᾶς διδάξει πάντα καὶ ὑπομνήσει[14] ὑμᾶς πάντα ἃ εἶπον ὑμῖν ἐγώ. **27.** <u>Εἰρήνην</u> ἀφίημι ὑμῖν, εἰρήνην τὴν ἐμὴν δίδωμι ὑμῖν· οὐ καθὼς ὁ κόσμος δίδωσιν ἐγὼ δίδωμι ὑμῖν. μὴ ταρασσέσθω[15] ὑμῶν ἡ καρδία μηδὲ δειλιάτω.[16]

28. ἠκούσατε ὅτι ἐγὼ εἶπον ὑμῖν, Ὑπάγω καὶ ἔρχομαι πρὸς ὑμᾶς. εἰ ἠγαπᾶτέ με <u>ἐχάρητε</u> ἄν, ὅτι πορεύομαι πρὸς τὸν πατέρα, ὅτι ὁ πατὴρ μείζων μού ἐστιν. **29.** καὶ νῦν εἴρηκα ὑμῖν πρὶν[17] γενέσθαι, ἵνα ὅταν <u>γένηται</u> πιστεύσητε. **30.** οὐκέτι πολλὰ λαλήσω μεθ᾽ ὑμῶν, ἔρχεται γὰρ ὁ τοῦ κόσμου ἄρχων· καὶ ἐν ἐμοὶ οὐκ ἔχει οὐδέν, **31.** ἀλλ᾽ ἵνα γνῷ ὁ κόσμος ὅτι ἀγαπῶ τὸν πατέρα, καὶ καθὼς ἐνετείλατο[18] μοι ὁ πατήρ, οὕτως ποιῶ. Ἐγείρεσθε, ἄγωμεν ἐντεῦθεν.[19]

Parsing: εἰρήνην _____

ἐχάρητε _____

γένηται _____

Translation: _____

_____

_____

_____

_____

_____

_____

_____

_____

_____

_____

_____

_____

_____

---

[13]See verse 15.   [14]ὑπομιμνήσκω, *I remember, remind* (7).   [15]See verse 1.   [16]δειλιάω, *I am cowardly, timid* (1).   [17]πρίν, *before* (13).   [18]ἐντέλλομαι, *I command* (15).   [19]ἐντεῦθεν, *from here, from this* (10).

Vocabulary

Friends	Memory Aids
διδαχή, -ῆς, ἡ, *teaching, instruction* (30).	Didache—a Christian *teaching* text.
δυνατός, -ή, -όν, *powerful, strong* (32).	δύναμις—power.
ἐγγύς, *near, close to* (31).	ἐγγίζω—I come *near*.
ἐκπορεύομαι, *I go out, come out* (33).	I *go* (πορεύομαι) *out* (ἐκ).
ἐλπίζω, *I hope, expect* (31).	ἐλπίς—*hope*, expectation.
ἐπικαλέω, *I call, invoke, appeal to* (30).	καλέω—I *call*.
ἱερεύς, -έως, ὁ, *priest* (31).	ἀρχιερεύς—high *priest*.
ὁμοίως, *likewise, similarly* (30).	ὅμοιος—like, of the same nature.
Cousins	
ἀκάθαρτος, -ον, *unclean, impure* (32).	Not (ἀ) clean (catharsis).
καθαρίζω, *I make clean, cleanse* (31).	Catharsis—a *cleansing*.
ἀναγινώσκω, *I read, read aloud* (32).	I know (γινώσκω) by *reading*.
ἄνεμος, -ου, ὁ, *wind* (31).	An anemometer measures *wind* speed.
ἥλιος, -ου, ὁ, *sun* (32).	Helios—the Greek god of the *sun*.
φυλάσσω, *I keep, guard, watch* (31).	I *guard* (φυλάσσω) the prison (φυλακή).
Strangers	
ἀγοράζω, *I buy, purchase* (30).	Agora—a Greek marketplace.
ἀρνίον, -ου, τό, *lamb, sheep* (30).	
διαθήκη, -ης, ἡ, *covenant, will, testament* (33).	
ἔξεστι, *it is lawful, it is permitted* (31).	Ecstasy *is permitted*.
ἐχθρός, -ά, -όν, *hostile, an enemy* (32).	
ναί, *yes, indeed* (33).	*Yes, indeed* we shall draw nigh (near).
παραγγέλλω, *I command, give orders* (32).	
παρρησία, -ας, ἡ, *boldness, confidence* (31).	παρά + ῥῆμα, speech alongside
πλῆθος, -ους, τό, *multitude, crowd* (31).	
πλήν, *however, but, except* (31).	*But* the plane, *however*, left on time.
ποῖος, -α, -ον, *of what kind? what?* (33).	*What* is your point?
ποτήριον, -ου, τό, *cup, drinking vessel* (31).	Use the *cup* to drink from the pot.
σκότος, -ους, τό, *darkness, gloom* (31).	Scoundrels skulk in the dark.
ὑπομονή, -ῆς, ἡ, *steadfast endurance, patience* (32).	To remain (μένω) under (ὑπό) takes *patience*.
φαίνω, *I shine, appear* (31).	It *appears* fine.
φυλή, -ῆς, ἡ, *tribe, nation* (31).	You would be a fool to join that *tribe*.

Week Seven

Matthew 26:27–63

Reading 1 | Matthew 26:27–31

27. καὶ λαβὼν ποτήριον καὶ εὐχαριστήσας ἔδωκεν αὐτοῖς λέγων, <u>Πίετε</u> ἐξ αὐτοῦ πάντες,
28. τοῦτο γάρ ἐστιν τὸ αἷμά μου τῆς <u>διαθήκης</u> τὸ περὶ πολλῶν ἐκχυννόμενον[1] εἰς ἄφεσιν[2]
ἁμαρτιῶν. **29.** λέγω δὲ ὑμῖν, οὐ μὴ πίω ἀπ᾽ ἄρτι ἐκ τούτου τοῦ γενήματος[3] τῆς ἀμπέλου[4] ἕως
τῆς ἡμέρας ἐκείνης ὅταν αὐτὸ πίνω μεθ᾽ ὑμῶν καινὸν ἐν τῇ βασιλείᾳ τοῦ πατρός μου.

30. Καὶ ὑμνήσαντες[5] ἐξῆλθον εἰς τὸ Ὄρος τῶν Ἐλαιῶν.[6]

31. Τότε λέγει αὐτοῖς ὁ Ἰησοῦς, Πάντες ὑμεῖς <u>σκανδαλισθήσεσθε</u> ἐν ἐμοὶ ἐν τῇ νυκτὶ
ταύτῃ, γέγραπται γάρ, Πατάξω[7] τὸν ποιμένα,[8] καὶ διασκορπισθήσονται[9] τὰ πρόβατα τῆς
ποίμνης.[10]

Parsing: πίετε

διαθήκης

σκανδαλισθήσεσθε

Translation:

---

[1] ἐκχέω, *I pour out, shed* [Vocab. 8].   [2] ἄφεσις, -εως, ἡ, *release, pardon* (17).   [3] γένημα, -ατος, τό, *fruit,
produce* (4).   [4] ἄμπελος, -ου, ἡ, *vine, grapevine* (9).   [5] ὑμνέω, *I sing hymns of praise, sing a hymn* (4).
[6] ἐλαία, -ας, ἡ, *olive tree, olive* (13).   [7] πατάσσω, *I strike, slay* (10).   [8] ποιμήν, -ένος, ὁ, *shepherd* (18).
[9] διασκορπίζω, *I scatter, disperse* (9).   [10] ποίμνη, -ης, ἡ, *flock* (5).

54

Reading 2 | Matthew 26:32–37

32. μετὰ δὲ τὸ ἐγερθῆναί με προάξω[11] ὑμᾶς εἰς τὴν Γαλιλαίαν.

33. ἀποκριθεὶς δὲ ὁ Πέτρος εἶπεν αὐτῷ, Εἰ πάντες σκανδαλισθήσονται ἐν σοί, ἐγὼ οὐδέποτε[12] σκανδαλισθήσομαι.

34. ἔφη αὐτῷ ὁ Ἰησοῦς, Ἀμὴν λέγω σοι ὅτι ἐν ταύτῃ τῇ νυκτὶ πρὶν[13] ἀλέκτορα[14] φωνῆσαι τρὶς ἀπαρνήσῃ[15] με.

35. λέγει αὐτῷ ὁ Πέτρος, Κἂν[16] δέῃ με σὺν σοὶ ἀποθανεῖν, οὐ μή σε ἀπαρνήσομαι. ὁμοίως καὶ πάντες οἱ μαθηταὶ εἶπαν.

36. Τότε ἔρχεται μετ' αὐτῶν ὁ Ἰησοῦς εἰς χωρίον[17] λεγόμενον Γεθσημανὶ[18] καὶ λέγει τοῖς μαθηταῖς, Καθίσατε αὐτοῦ[19] ἕως οὗ ἀπελθὼν ἐκεῖ προσεύξωμαι. **37.** καὶ παραλαβὼν τὸν Πέτρον καὶ τοὺς δύο υἱοὺς Ζεβεδαίου[20] ἤρξατο λυπεῖσθαι[21] καὶ ἀδημονεῖν.[22]

Parsing: ἔφη _____

φωνῆσαι _____

δέῃ _____

Translation: _____

_____

_____

_____

_____

_____

_____

_____

_____

_____

_____

_____

_____

---

[11]προάγω, *I lead forward, go or come before* [Vocab. 12].   [12]οὐδέποτε, *never* (16).   [13]πρὶν, *before* (13). πρὶν + infinitive denotes subsequent time. Translate it as *before* + finite verb (Wallace, 596).   [14]ἀλέκτωρ, -ορος, ὁ, *cock, rooster* (13).   [15]ἀπαρνέομαι, *I deny, reject* (11).   [16]κἂν, *and if, even if* (17).   [17]χωρίον, -ου, τό, *place, spot* (10).   [18]Γεθσημανί, *Gethsemane* (2).   [19]αὐτοῦ, this is an adverb that means *here, there* (4).   [20]Ζεβεδαῖος, -ου, ὁ, *Zebedee* (12).   [21]λυπέω, *I grieve, pain* [Vocab. 8].   [22]ἀδημονέω, *I am distressed, troubled* (3).

Reading 3 | Matthew 26:38–43

38. τότε λέγει αὐτοῖς, Περίλυπός²³ ἐστιν ἡ ψυχή μου ἕως²⁴ θανάτου· μείνατε ὧδε καὶ γρηγορεῖτε²⁵ μετ᾽ ἐμοῦ.

39. καὶ προελθὼν μικρὸν <u>ἔπεσεν</u> ἐπὶ πρόσωπον αὐτοῦ προσευχόμενος καὶ λέγων, Πάτερ μου, εἰ δυνατόν ἐστιν, παρελθάτω ἀπ᾽ ἐμοῦ τὸ ποτήριον τοῦτο· πλὴν οὐχ ὡς ἐγὼ θέλω ἀλλ᾽ ὡς σύ.

40. καὶ ἔρχεται πρὸς τοὺς μαθητὰς καὶ εὑρίσκει αὐτοὺς καθεύδοντας,²⁶ καὶ λέγει τῷ Πέτρῳ, Οὕτως οὐκ ἰσχύσατε μίαν ὥραν γρηγορῆσαι μετ᾽ ἐμου; **41.** γρηγορεῖτε καὶ <u>προσεύχεσθε</u>, ἵνα μὴ εἰσέλθητε εἰς πειρασμόν·²⁷ τὸ μὲν πνεῦμα πρόθυμον²⁸ ἡ δὲ σὰρξ ἀσθενής.²⁹

42. πάλιν ἐκ δευτέρου ἀπελθὼν προσηύξατο λέγων, Πάτερ μου, εἰ οὐ δύναται τοῦτο <u>παρελθεῖν</u> ἐὰν μὴ αὐτὸ πίω, γενηθήτω τὸ θέλημά σου.

43. καὶ ἐλθὼν πάλιν εὗρεν αὐτοὺς καθεύδοντας, ἦσαν γὰρ αὐτῶν οἱ ὀφθαλμοὶ βεβαρημένοι.³⁰

Parsing:	ἔπεσεν	
	προσεύχεσθε	
	παρελθεῖν	

Translation:

---

²³περίλυπος, -ον, *very sad, deeply grieved* (5).   ²⁴ἕως is serving as an improper preposition—translate as *unto* (BAGD, s.v. ἕως, II.4).   ²⁵γρηγορέω, *I am awake, am watchful* [Vocab. 11].   ²⁶καθεύδω, *I sleep* [Vocab. 11]. ²⁷πειρασμός, -οῦ, ὁ, *temptation, test* [Vocab. 12].   ²⁸πρόθυμος, -ον, *ready, willing* (3).   ²⁹ἀσθενής, -ές, *weak, powerless, sick* [Vocab. 8].   ³⁰βαρέω, *I weigh down, burden* (6).

Reading 4 | Matthew 26:44–49

44. καὶ ἀφεὶς αὐτοὺς πάλιν ἀπελθὼν προσηύξατο ἐκ τρίτου τὸν αὐτὸν λόγον εἰπὼν πάλιν.

45. τότε ἔρχεται πρὸς τοὺς μαθητὰς καὶ λέγει αὐτοῖς, Καθεύδετε[31] τὸ λοιπὸν[32] καὶ ἀναπαύεσθε;[33] ἰδοὺ <u>ἤγγικεν</u> ἡ ὥρα καὶ ὁ υἱὸς τοῦ ἀνθρώπου <u>παραδίδοται</u> εἰς χεῖρας ἁμαρτωλῶν. **46.** ἐγείρεσθε, ἄγωμεν· ἰδοὺ ἤγγικεν ὁ παραδιδούς με.

47. Καὶ ἔτι αὐτοῦ λαλοῦντος ἰδοὺ Ἰούδας εἷς τῶν δώδεκα ἦλθεν καὶ μετ᾽ αὐτοῦ ὄχλος πολὺς μετὰ μαχαιρῶν καὶ ξύλων[34] ἀπὸ τῶν ἀρχιερέων καὶ πρεσβυτέρων τοῦ λαοῦ. **48.** ὁ δὲ παραδιδοὺς αὐτὸν ἔδωκεν αὐτοῖς σημεῖον λέγων, Ὃν ἂν φιλήσω[35] αὐτός ἐστιν· κρατήσατε αὐτόν. **49.** καὶ εὐθέως προσελθὼν τῷ Ἰησοῦ εἶπεν, <u>Χαῖρε</u>, ῥαββί·[36] καὶ κατεφίλησεν[37] αὐτόν.

Parsing: ἤγγικεν _____

παραδίδοται _____

χαῖρε _____

Translation: _____

_____

_____

_____

_____

_____

_____

_____

_____

_____

_____

_____

_____

_____

_____

_____

---

[31]See verse 40. [32]λοιπός is used adverbially here (in the neut.). Translate it as *are you still* (BAGD s.v. λοιπός, 3.a.α.) [33]ἀναπαύω, *I cause to rest, rest* (mid) (12). [34]ξύλον, -ου, τό, *wood, tree, club* [Vocab. 12].
[35]φιλέω, *I love, kiss* [Vocab. 9]. [36]ῥαββί, *rabbi* (15). [37]καταφιλέω, *I kiss* (6).

Reading 5 | Matthew 26:50–56

50. ὁ δὲ Ἰησοῦς εἶπεν αὐτῷ, Ἑταῖρε,[38] ἐφ᾽ ὃ πάρει.[39] τότε προσελθόντες ἐπέβαλον[40] τὰς χεῖρας ἐπὶ τὸν Ἰησοῦν καὶ ἐκράτησαν αὐτόν. **51.** καὶ ἰδοὺ εἷς τῶν μετὰ Ἰησοῦ ἐκτείνας[41] τὴν χεῖρα ἀπέσπασεν[42] τὴν μάχαιραν αὐτοῦ καὶ πατάξας[43] τὸν δοῦλον τοῦ ἀρχιερέως ἀφεῖλεν[44] αὐτοῦ τὸ ὠτίον.[45]

52. τότε λέγει αὐτῷ ὁ Ἰησοῦς, Ἀπόστρεψον[46] τὴν μάχαιράν σου εἰς τὸν τόπον αὐτῆς· πάντες γὰρ οἱ λαβόντες μάχαιραν ἐν μαχαίρῃ <u>ἀπολοῦνται</u>. **53.** ἢ δοκεῖς ὅτι οὐ δύναμαι παρακαλέσαι τὸν πατέρα μου, καὶ <u>παραστήσει</u> μοι ἄρτι πλείω[47] δώδεκα λεγιῶνας[48] ἀγγέλων· **54.** πῶς οὖν πληρωθῶσιν αἱ γραφαὶ ὅτι οὕτως δεῖ γενέσθαι;

55. Ἐν ἐκείνῃ τῇ ὥρᾳ εἶπεν ὁ Ἰησοῦς τοῖς ὄχλοις, Ὡς ἐπὶ λῃστὴν[49] ἐξήλθατε μετὰ μαχαιρῶν καὶ ξύλων[50] συλλαβεῖν[51] με; καθ᾽ ἡμέραν[52] ἐν τῷ ἱερῷ ἐκαθεζόμην διδάσκων καὶ οὐκ ἐκρατήσατέ με. **56.** τοῦτο δὲ ὅλον γέγονεν ἵνα <u>πληρωθῶσιν</u> αἱ γραφαὶ τῶν προφητῶν. Τότε οἱ μαθηταὶ πάντες ἀφέντες αὐτὸν ἔφυγον.

Parsing: ἀπολοῦνται _____

παραστήσει _____

πληρωθῶσιν _____

Translation: _____

_____

_____

_____

_____

_____

_____

_____

_____

_____

---

[38]ἑταῖρος, -ου, ὁ, _friend, companion_ (3). This word is in the vocative case (_BBG_, 105).   [39]πάρειμι, _I am present, have come_ [Vocab. 10].   [40]ἐπιβάλλω, _I throw over, lay on_ (18).   [41]ἐκτείνω, _I stretch out_ (16).   [42]ἀποσπάω, _I draw away, pull away_ (4).   [43]See verse 31.   [44]ἀφαιρέω, _I take away, cut off_ (10).   [45]ὠτίον, -ου, τό, _ear_ (3). [46]ἀποστρέφω, _I turn away, return_ (9).   [47]This is a comparative adjective derived from πολύς. Translate it as _more [than]_ (BAGD, s.v. πόλυς, II.2.c).   [48]λεγιών, -ῶνος, ἡ, _legion_ (4).   [49]λῃστής, -οῦ, ὁ, _robber, bandit_ (15).   [50]See verse 47.   [51]συλλαμβάνω, _I arrest, catch_ (16).   [52]Translate καθ᾽ ἡμέραν as _daily_ (see BAGD, s.v. κατά, II.2.c).

Reading 6 | Matthew 26:57–63

57. Οἱ δὲ <u>κρατήσαντες</u> τὸν Ἰησοῦν ἀπήγαγον[53] πρὸς Καϊάφαν[54] τὸν ἀρχιερέα, ὅπου οἱ γραμματεῖς καὶ οἱ πρεσβύτεροι <u>συνήχθησαν</u>. **58.** ὁ δὲ Πέτρος ἠκολούθει αὐτῷ ἀπὸ μακρόθεν[55] ἕως τῆς αὐλῆς[56] τοῦ ἀρχιερέως, καὶ εἰσελθὼν ἔσω[57] ἐκάθητο μετὰ τῶν ὑπηρετῶν[58] ἰδεῖν τὸ τέλος.

59. οἱ δὲ ἀρχιερεῖς καὶ τὸ συνέδριον[59] ὅλον ἐζήτουν ψευδομαρτυρίαν[60] κατὰ τοῦ Ἰησοῦ ὅπως αὐτὸν θανατώσωσιν,[61] **60.** καὶ οὐχ εὗρον πολλῶν προσελθόντων ψευδομαρτύρων. ὕστερον[62] δὲ προσελθόντες δύο **61.** εἶπαν, Οὗτος ἔφη, Δύναμαι καταλῦσαι[63] τὸν ναὸν τοῦ θεοῦ καὶ διὰ <u>τριῶν</u> ἡμερῶν οἰκοδομῆσαι.

62. καὶ ἀναστὰς ὁ ἀρχιερεὺς εἶπεν αὐτῷ, Οὐδὲν ἀποκρίνῃ τί οὗτοί σου καταμαρτυροῦσιν;[64] **63.** ὁ δὲ Ἰησοῦς ἐσιώπα.[65] καὶ ὁ ἀρχιερεὺς εἶπεν αὐτῷ, Ἐξορκίζω[66] σε κατὰ τοῦ θεοῦ τοῦ ζῶντος ἵνα ἡμῖν εἴπῃς εἰ σὺ εἶ ὁ Χριστὸς ὁ υἱὸς τοῦ θεοῦ.

Parsing: κρατήσαντες _____

συνήχθησαν _____

τριῶν _____

Translation: _____

_____

_____

_____

_____

_____

_____

_____

_____

_____

_____

---

[53]ἀπάγω, *I lead away, bring away* (15).   [54]Καϊάφας, α, ὁ, *Caiaphas* (9).   [55]μακρόθεν, *from a distance, far off* (14).   [56]αὐλή, -ῆς, ἡ, *courtyard, palace* (12).   [57]ἔσω, *in, inside* (9).   [58]ὑπηρέτης, -ου, ὁ, *servant, assistant* [Vocab. 12].   [59]συνέδριον, -ου, τό, *Sanhedrin, council* [Vocab. 11].   [60]ψευδομαρτυρία, -ας, ἡ, *false witness, false testimony* (2).   [61]θανατόω, *I put to death, kill* (11).   [62]ὕστερος, -α, -ον, *later, last* (12).   [63]καταλύω, *I throw down, tear down* (17).   [64]καταμαρτυρέω, *I bear witness against, testify against* (3).   [65]σιωπάω, *I keep silent, am quiet* (10).   [66]ἐξορκίζω, *I adjure, put under oath* (1).

Vocabulary

Friends	Memory Aids
ἁγιάζω, *I make holy, sanctify* (28).	ἅγιος—**holy**.
ἀληθινός, -ή, -όν, *true* (28).	ἀλήθεια—truth.
Βαρναβᾶς, -ᾶ, ὁ, *Barnabas* (28).	Just like it sounds.
γνῶσις, -εως, ἡ, *knowledge, wisdom* (29).	γινώσκω—I know.
διάκονος, -ου, ὁ, ἡ, *servant, deacon* (29).	**Deacon**.
Ἠλίας, -ου, ὁ, *Elijah* (29).	Just like it sounds.
ἴδε, *look, see, behold* (29).	ἰδού—**look**.
Καῖσαρ, -ος, ὁ, *Caesar, emperor* (29).	Just like it sounds.
παρέρχομαι, *I go or pass by, come* (29).	I *go* (ἔρχομαι) beside (παρά).
προσκαλέω, *I summon, call to myself* (29).	I *call* (καλέω) *to* (πρός).
σκανδαλίζω, *I stumble, cause to fall, take offense* (29).	Scandalize—to cause **offense**.
συνέρχομαι, *I come together* (30).	I *come* (ἔρχομαι) **together** with (σύν).

Cousins	
ἀδικέω, *I wrong, do wrong* (28).	I do not (ἀ) do righteousness (δικαιοσύνη).
ἡγέομαι, *I lead, guide, rule* (28).	Hegemony—leadership or domination.
παράκλησις, -εως, ἡ, *encouragement, consolation* (29).	Paraclete—the Holy Spirit, our *encourager*.
φίλος, -η, -ον, *beloved, loving, friend* (29).	Philadelphia—city of brotherly *love*.

Strangers	
γαμέω, *I marry* (28).	Marriage can be a gamble.
ἐλεέω, *I have mercy, am merciful* (29).	Latin: Kyrie eleison—Lord **have mercy**!
ἐπιτιμάω, *I rebuke, warn* (29).	
θυγάτηρ, -τρος, ἡ, *daughter, girl* (28).	A thug-got-her, my ***daughter***!
θυσία, -ας, ἡ, *sacrifice, offering* (28).	They were enthused to make a **sacrifice**.
ἰσχυρός, -ά, -όν, *strong, mighty* (29).	Learn these two together.
ἰσχύω, *I am strong, powerful* (28).	
μάχαιρα, -ης, ἡ, *sword* (29).	Machairodus—Saber-toothed tiger.
μισθός, -οῦ, ὁ, *pay, wages, reward* (29).	I had a mis-thought about my *pay*.
πάσχα, τό, *Passover, Passover meal* (29).	At *Passover* we eat the paschal lamb.
πόθεν, *from where? whence?* (29).	
ποτέ, *at some time, formerly* (29).	Potent? It was ***formerly***.
συνείδησις, -εως, ἡ, *conscience, consciousness* (30).	
φεύγω, *I flee, escape* (29).	I *escaped* the feud.

Week Eight
Matthew 22:20–23:13

Reading 1 | Matthew 22:20–25

20. καὶ λέγει αὐτοῖς, Τίνος ἡ εἰκών[1] αὕτη καὶ ἡ ἐπιγραφή;[2]

21. λέγουσιν αὐτῷ, Καίσαρος. τότε λέγει αὐτοῖς, Ἀπόδοτε οὖν τὰ Καίσαρος Καίσαρι καὶ τὰ τοῦ θεοῦ τῷ θεῷ.

22. καὶ ἀκούσαντες ἐθαύμασαν, καὶ ἀφέντες αὐτὸν ἀπῆλθαν.

23. Ἐν ἐκείνῃ τῇ ἡμέρᾳ προσῆλθον αὐτῷ Σαδδουκαῖοι,[3] λέγοντες μὴ εἶναι ἀνάστασιν, καὶ ἐπηρώτησαν αὐτὸν **24.** λέγοντες, Διδάσκαλε, Μωϋσῆς εἶπεν, Ἐάν τις ἀποθάνῃ μὴ ἔχων τέκνα, ἐπιγαμβρεύσει[4] ὁ ἀδελφὸς αὐτοῦ τὴν γυναῖκα αὐτοῦ καὶ ἀναστήσει σπέρμα τῷ ἀδελφῷ αὐτοῦ. **25.** ἦσαν δὲ παρ᾽ ἡμῖν ἑπτὰ ἀδελφοί· καὶ ὁ πρῶτος γήμας ἐτελεύτησεν,[5] καὶ μὴ ἔχων σπέρμα ἀφῆκεν τὴν γυναῖκα αὐτοῦ τῷ ἀδελφῷ αὐτοῦ·

Parsing: ἀπόδοτε   _____

   ἀποθάνῃ   _____

   γήμας   _____

Translation: _____

_____

_____

_____

_____

_____

_____

_____

_____

_____

---

[1]εἰκών, -όνος, ἡ, *image, likeness* [Vocab. 10].   [2]ἐπιγραφή, -ῆς, ἡ, *inscription, superscription* (5).   [3]Σαδδουκαῖος, -ου, ὁ, *Sadducee*, (14).   [4]ἐπιγαμβρεύω, *I marry as next of kin* (1).   [5]τελευτάω, *I come to an end, die* (11).

Reading 2 | **Matthew 22:26–33**

26. ὁμοίως καὶ ὁ δεύτερος καὶ ὁ τρίτος, ἕως τῶν ἑπτά. **27.** ὕστερον[6] δὲ πάντων <u>ἀπέθανεν</u> ἡ γυνή. **28.** ἐν τῇ ἀναστάσει οὖν τίνος τῶν ἑπτὰ ἔσται γυνή; πάντες γὰρ ἔσχον αὐτήν.

29. ἀποκριθεὶς δὲ ὁ Ἰησοῦς εἶπεν αὐτοῖς, <u>Πλανᾶσθε</u> μὴ εἰδότες τὰς γραφὰς μηδὲ τὴν δύναμιν τοῦ θεοῦ· **30.** ἐν γὰρ τῇ ἀναστάσει οὔτε γαμοῦσιν οὔτε γαμίζονται,[7] ἀλλ᾽ ὡς ἄγγελοι ἐν τῷ οὐρανῷ εἰσιν. **31.** περὶ δὲ τῆς ἀναστάσεως τῶν νεκρῶν οὐκ ἀνέγνωτε τὸ <u>ῥηθὲν</u> ὑμῖν ὑπὸ τοῦ θεοῦ λέγοντος, **32.** Ἐγώ εἰμι ὁ θεὸς Ἀβραὰμ καὶ ὁ θεὸς Ἰσαὰκ[8] καὶ ὁ θεὸς Ἰακώβ; οὐκ ἔστιν ὁ θεὸς νεκρῶν ἀλλὰ ζώντων.

33. καὶ ἀκούσαντες οἱ ὄχλοι ἐξεπλήσσοντο[9] ἐπὶ τῇ διδαχῇ αὐτοῦ.

Parsing: ἀπέθανεν _____

πλανᾶσθε _____

ῥηθὲν _____

Translation:

_____

_____

_____

_____

_____

_____

_____

_____

_____

_____

_____

_____

_____

---

[6]ὕστερος, -α, -ον, _latter, last_ (12).   [7]γαμίζω, _I give in marriage, marry_ (7).   [8]Ἰσαάκ, ὁ, _Isaac_ [Vocab. 12].
[9]ἐκπλήσσω, _I am amazed, overwhelmed_ (13).

Reading 3 | **Matthew 22:34–40**

34. Οἱ δὲ Φαρισαῖοι ἀκούσαντες ὅτι ἐφίμωσεν[10] τοὺς Σαδδουκαίους[11] συνήχθησαν ἐπὶ τὸ αὐτό. **35.** καὶ ἐπηρώτησεν εἷς ἐξ αὐτῶν νομικὸς[12] πειράζων αὐτόν, **36.** <u>Διδάσκαλε</u>, ποία ἐντολὴ μεγάλη ἐν τῷ νόμῳ;

37. ὁ δὲ ἔφη αὐτῷ, <u>Ἀγαπήσεις</u> κύριον τὸν θεόν σου ἐν ὅλῃ τῇ καρδίᾳ σου καὶ ἐν <u>ὅλῃ</u> τῇ ψυχῇ σου καὶ ἐν ὅλῃ τῇ διανοίᾳ[13] σου· **38.** αὕτη ἐστὶν ἡ μεγάλη καὶ πρώτη ἐντολή. **39.** δευτέρα δὲ ὁμοία αὐτῇ, Ἀγαπήσεις τὸν πλησίον[14] σου ὡς σεαυτόν. **40.** ἐν ταύταις ταῖς δυσὶν ἐντολαῖς ὅλος ὁ νόμος κρέμαται[15] καὶ οἱ προφῆται.

Parsing: διδάσκαλε _____
ἀγαπήσεις _____
ὅλη _____

Translation:

_____

[10]φιμόω, *I muzzle, silence* (7). [11]See verse 23. [12]νομικός, -ή, -όν, *legal expert, lawyer* (9). [13]διάνοια, -ας, ἡ, *mind, thought, understanding* (12). [14]πλησίον, *near, close by* (when used as a subst., *neighbor, fellow*) (17). [15]κρεμάννυμι, *I hang, crucify, depend* (7).

Reading 4 | Matthew 22:41–46

41. <u>Συνηγμένων</u> δὲ τῶν Φαρισαίων ἐπηρώτησεν αὐτοὺς ὁ Ἰησοῦς **42.** λέγων, Τί ὑμῖν δοκεῖ περὶ τοῦ Χριστοῦ; τίνος υἱός ἐστιν; λέγουσιν αὐτῷ, Τοῦ Δαυίδ.

43. λέγει αὐτοῖς, Πῶς οὖν Δαυὶδ ἐν πνεύματι καλεῖ αὐτὸν κύριον λέγων,

44. Εἶπεν κύριος τῷ κυρίῳ μου, Κάθου ἐκ δεξιῶν μου ἕως ἂν <u>θῶ</u> τοὺς ἐχθρούς σου ὑποκάτω[16] τῶν ποδῶν σου;

45. εἰ οὖν Δαυὶδ καλεῖ αὐτὸν κύριον, πῶς υἱὸς αὐτοῦ ἐστιν; **46.** καὶ οὐδεὶς ἐδύνατο ἀποκριθῆναι αὐτῷ λόγον οὐδὲ ἐτόλμησέν[17] τις ἀπ᾽ ἐκείνης τῆς ἡμέρας <u>ἐπερωτῆσαι</u> αὐτὸν οὐκέτι.

Parsing: συνηγμένων   ....

                  θῶ   ....

                  ἐπερωτῆσαι   ....

Translation: ....

---

[16]ὑποκάτω, *under, below* (11).   [17]τολμάω, *I dare, bring myself* (16).

Reading 5 | Matthew 23:1–7

1. Τότε ὁ Ἰησοῦς ἐλάλησεν τοῖς ὄχλοις καὶ τοῖς μαθηταῖς αὐτοῦ **2.** λέγων, Ἐπὶ τῆς Μωϋσέως καθέδρας[18] ἐκάθισαν οἱ γραμματεῖς καὶ οἱ Φαρισαῖοι. **3.** πάντα οὖν ὅσα ἐὰν εἴπωσιν ὑμῖν ποιήσατε καὶ τηρεῖτε, κατὰ δὲ τὰ ἔργα αὐτῶν μὴ ποιεῖτε· λέγουσιν γὰρ καὶ οὐ ποιοῦσιν. **4.** δεσμεύουσιν[19] δὲ φορτία[20] βαρέα[21] καὶ ἐπιτιθέασιν ἐπὶ τοὺς ὤμους[22] τῶν ἀνθρώπων, αὐτοὶ δὲ τῷ δακτύλῳ[23] αὐτῶν οὐ θέλουσιν κινῆσαι[24] αὐτά.

5. πάντα δὲ τὰ ἔργα αὐτῶν ποιοῦσιν πρὸς τὸ θεαθῆναι[25] τοῖς ἀνθρώποις· πλατύνουσιν[26] γὰρ τὰ φυλακτήρια[27] αὐτῶν καὶ μεγαλύνουσιν[28] τὰ κράσπεδα[29] τῶν ἱματίων αὐτῶν, **6.** φιλοῦσιν δὲ τὴν πρωτοκλισίαν[30] ἐν τοῖς δείπνοις[31] καὶ τὰς πρωτοκαθεδρίας[32] ἐν ταῖς συναγωγαῖς **7.** καὶ τοὺς ἀσπασμοὺς[33] ἐν ταῖς ἀγοραῖς[34] καὶ καλεῖσθαι ὑπὸ τῶν ἀνθρώπων, Ῥαββί.[35]

Parsing: εἴπωσιν _____

φιλοῦσιν _____

καλεῖσθαι _____

Translation: _____

_____

_____

_____

_____

_____

_____

_____

_____

_____

_____

_____

---

[18]καθέδρα, -ας, ἡ, _chair, seat_ (3).   [19]δεσμεύω, _I bind, tie up_ (3).   [20]φορτίον, -ου, τό, _burden, load_ (6).
[21]βαρύς, -εῖα, -ύ, _heavy, burdensome_ (6).   [22]ὦμος, -ου, ὁ, _shoulder_ (2).   [23]δάκτυλος, -ου, ὁ, _finger_ (8).
[24]κινέω, _I move, remove_ (8).   [25]θεάομαι, _I see, look at_ [Vocab. 11].   [26]πλατύνω, _I make broad, wide, enlarge_ (3).   [27]φυλακτήριον, -ου, τό, _phylactery_ (1).   [28]μεγαλύνω, _I make large or long_ (8).
[29]κράσπεδον, -ου, τό, _edge, tassel_ (5).   [30]πρωτοκλισία, -ας, ἡ, _place of honor_ (5).   [31]δεῖπνον, -ου, τό, _dinner, banquet_ (16).   [32]πρωτοκαθεδρία, -ας, ἡ, _place of honor, best seat_ (4).   [33]ἀσπασμός, -οῦ, ὁ, _greeting_ (10).   [34]ἀγορά, -ᾶς, ἡ, _marketplace_ (11).   [35]ῥαββί, _rabbi, teacher_ (15).

Reading 6 | Matthew 23:8–13

8. ὑμεῖς δὲ μὴ <u>κληθῆτε</u>, ῥαββι, εἷς γάρ ἐστιν ὑμῶν ὁ διδάσκαλος, πάντες δὲ ὑμεῖς ἀδελφοί ἐστε. **9.** καὶ πατέρα μὴ <u>καλέσητε</u> ὑμῶν ἐπὶ τῆς γῆς, εἷς γάρ ἐστιν ὑμῶν ὁ πατὴρ ὁ οὐράνιος.[36] **10.** μηδὲ κληθῆτε καθηγηταί,[37] ὅτι καθηγητὴς ὑμῶν ἐστιν εἷς ὁ Χριστός. **11.** ὁ δὲ μείζων ὑμῶν ἔσται ὑμῶν διάκονος. **12.** ὅστις δὲ ὑψώσει[38] ἑαυτὸν ταπεινωθήσεται[39] καὶ ὅστις ταπεινώσει ἑαυτὸν ὑψωθήσεται.

13. Οὐαὶ δὲ ὑμῖν, γραμματεῖς καὶ Φαρισαῖοι ὑποκριταί,[40] ὅτι κλείετε[41] τὴν βασιλείαν τῶν οὐρανῶν ἔμπροσθεν τῶν ἀνθρώπων· ὑμεῖς γὰρ οὐκ εἰσέρχεσθε οὐδὲ τοὺς εἰσερχομένους <u>ἀφίετε</u> εἰσελθεῖν.

Parsing: κληθῆτε _____

καλέσητε _____

ἀφίετε _____

Translation: _____

_____

_____

_____

_____

_____

_____

_____

_____

_____

_____

_____

_____

---

[36]οὐράνιος, -ον, _heavenly_ (9).   [37]καθηγητής, -οῦ, ὁ, _teacher_ (2).   [38]ὑψόω, _I lift up, exalt_ [Vocab. 12].
[39]ταπεινόω, _I lower, humble_ (14).   [40]ὑποκριτής, -οῦ, ὁ, _hypocrite, pretender_ (17).   [41]κλείω, _I shut, lock, bar_ (16).

Vocabulary

Friends	Memory Aids
ἀδελφή, -ῆς, ἡ, *sister* (26).	ἀδελφός—brother.
ἀληθής, -ές, *true, real* (26).	ἀλήθεια—truth.
ἀσθενής, -ές, *weak, powerless, sick* (26).	ἀσθενέω—I am **weak**
ἔλεος, -ους, τό, *pity, mercy* (27).	ἐλεέω—I have **mercy.**
Ἰακώβ, ὁ, *Jacob* (27).	Pronounce the *I* as an English *J*.
καθαρός, -ά, -όν, *clean, pure* (27).	ἀκάθαρτος—unclean.
Μαρία, -ας, ἡ, *Mary* (27).	Just like it sounds.
Μαριάμ, ἡ, *Mary, Miriam* (27).	Just like it sounds.
μυστήριον, -ου, τό, *mystery, secret* (28).	Almost like it sounds.
προφητεύω, *I prophesy* (28).	προφητεία—prophecy.
σταυρός, -οῦ, ὁ, *cross* (27).	σταυρόω—I crucify.
τελέω, *I finish, fulfill* (28).	τέλος—end (I reach the end, or finish).

Cousins	
ἀποκαλύπτω, *I reveal, uncover* (26).	All will be **revealed** at the apocalypse.
κώμη, -ης, ἡ, *village, town* (27).	Community.
πόσος, -η, -ον, *how great? how much?* (27).	ὅσος—**how great,** as great.
σός, σή, σόν, *your, yours* (27).	σύ—you.

Strangers	
βαστάζω, *I bear, endure, carry, comprehend* (27).	I **endured** the bastinado (a beating).
ἐκχέω, *I pour out, shed* (27).	An echo **poured out** of the cave.
ἐνδύω, *I put on, clothe* (27).	I endue you with **clothes.**
ἕνεκα, *because of, on account of* (26).	You must have an enema **on account of** (ἕνεκα) your illness.
ἐπεί, *because, since* (26).	
ἥκω, *I have come, am present* (26).	I **have come** (ἥκω) to hear the echo.
ἰάομαι, *I heal, cure* (26).	Psychiatrist—a **healer** of the psyche.
καταργέω, *I abolish* (27).	I categorically **abolished it.**
κρίμα, -ατος, τό, *judgment, decision* (27).	A criminal requires **judgment.**
λυπέω, *I grieve, pain* (26).	The lupus (wolf) was in **pain.**
νικάω, *I overcome, conquer, prevail* (28).	Nick will **conquer!**
ὀμνύω, *I swear, take an oath* (26).	
πλούσιος, -α, -ον, *rich, wealthy* (28).	A **rich** man has plus stuff.
χώρα, -ας, ἡ, *country, land* (28).	Cora lives in the **country.**

Week Nine

John 6:60–7:24

Reading 1 | John 6:60–65

60. Πολλοὶ οὖν ἀκούσαντες ἐκ τῶν μαθητῶν αὐτοῦ εἶπαν, Σκληρός[1] ἐστιν ὁ λόγος οὗτος· τίς δύναται αὐτοῦ ἀκούειν;

61. εἰδὼς δὲ ὁ Ἰησοῦς ἐν ἑαυτῷ ὅτι γογγύζουσιν[2] περὶ τούτου οἱ μαθηταὶ αὐτοῦ εἶπεν αὐτοῖς, Τοῦτο ὑμᾶς σκανδαλίζει; **62.** ἐὰν οὖν θεωρῆτε τὸν υἱὸν τοῦ ἀνθρώπου ἀναβαίνοντα ὅπου ἦν τὸ πρότερον;[3] **63.** τὸ πνεῦμά ἐστιν τὸ ζῳοποιοῦν,[4] ἡ σὰρξ οὐκ ὠφελεῖ[5] οὐδέν· τὰ ῥήματα ἃ ἐγὼ λελάληκα ὑμῖν πνεῦμά ἐστιν καὶ ζωή ἐστιν. **64.** ἀλλ᾽ εἰσὶν ἐξ ὑμῶν τινες οἳ οὐ πιστεύουσιν. ᾔδει[6] γὰρ ἐξ ἀρχῆς ὁ Ἰησοῦς τίνες εἰσὶν οἱ μὴ πιστεύοντες καὶ τίς ἐστιν ὁ παραδώσων αὐτόν. **65.** καὶ ἔλεγεν, Διὰ τοῦτο εἴρηκα ὑμῖν ὅτι οὐδεὶς δύναται ἐλθεῖν πρός με ἐὰν μὴ ᾖ δεδομένον αὐτῷ ἐκ τοῦ πατρός.

Parsing: εἰδὼς   ....
              εἴρηκα   ....
              δεδομένον   ....

Translation: ....

....

....

....

....

....

....

....

....

---

[1]σκληρός, -ά, -όν, *hard, rough* (5).   [2]γογγύζω, *I grumble, mutter* (8).   [3]πρότερος, -α, -ον, *before, former, earlier* (11).   [4]ζῳοποιέω, *I make alive, quicken, give life to* (11).   [5]ὠφελέω, *I help, benefit* (15).   [6]This is the pluperfect form of οἶδα. Translate it as *he knew* (see *BBG*, 232; Wallace, 586).

Reading 2 | **John 6:66–71**

66. Ἐκ τούτου πολλοὶ ἐκ τῶν μαθητῶν αὐτοῦ ἀπῆλθον εἰς τὰ ὀπίσω καὶ οὐκέτι μετ᾿ αὐτοῦ <u>περιεπάτουν</u>.

67. εἶπεν οὖν ὁ Ἰησοῦς τοῖς δώδεκα, Μὴ καὶ ὑμεῖς θέλετε ὑπάγειν;

68. ἀπεκρίθη αὐτῷ Σίμων Πέτρος, Κύριε, πρὸς τίνα <u>ἀπελευσόμεθα</u>; ῥήματα ζωῆς αἰωνίου ἔχεις, **69.** καὶ ἡμεῖς πεπιστεύκαμεν καὶ ἐγνώκαμεν ὅτι σὺ εἶ ὁ ἅγιος τοῦ θεοῦ.

70. ἀπεκρίθη αὐτοῖς ὁ Ἰησοῦς, Οὐκ ἐγὼ ὑμᾶς τοὺς δώδεκα ἐξελεξάμην,[7] καὶ ἐξ ὑμῶν εἷς διάβολός ἐστιν; **71.** ἔλεγεν δὲ τὸν Ἰούδαν Σίμωνος Ἰσκαριώτου·[8] οὗτος γὰρ <u>ἔμελλεν</u> παραδιδόναι αὐτόν, εἷς ὢν ἐκ τῶν δώδεκα.

Parsing: περιεπάτουν _____

ἀπελευσόμεθα _____

ἔμελλεν _____

Translation: _____

_____

_____

_____

_____

_____

_____

_____

_____

_____

_____

_____

_____

_____

_____

[7]ἐκλέγομαι, *I choose, select* [Vocab. 11].   [8]Ἰσκαριώτης, -ου, ὁ, *Iscariot* (8).

Reading 3 | John 7:1–7

1. Καὶ μετὰ ταῦτα περιεπάτει ὁ Ἰησοῦς ἐν τῇ Γαλιλαίᾳ· οὐ γὰρ <u>ἤθελεν</u> ἐν τῇ Ἰουδαίᾳ περιπατεῖν, ὅτι ἐζήτουν αὐτὸν οἱ Ἰουδαῖοι ἀποκτεῖναι. **2.** ἦν δὲ ἐγγὺς ἡ ἑορτὴ τῶν Ἰουδαίων ἡ σκηνοπηγία.[9] **3.** <u>εἶπον</u> οὖν πρὸς αὐτὸν οἱ ἀδελφοὶ αὐτοῦ, Μετάβηθι[10] ἐντεῦθεν[11] καὶ ὕπαγε εἰς τὴν Ἰουδαίαν, ἵνα καὶ οἱ μαθηταί σου θεωρήσουσιν τὰ ἔργα ἃ ποιεῖς· **4.** οὐδεὶς γάρ τι ἐν κρυπτῷ[12] ποιεῖ καὶ ζητεῖ αὐτὸς ἐν παρρησίᾳ εἶναι. εἰ ταῦτα ποιεῖς, φανέρωσον σεαυτὸν τῷ κόσμῳ. **5.** οὐδὲ γὰρ οἱ ἀδελφοὶ αὐτοῦ ἐπίστευον εἰς αὐτόν.

6. λέγει οὖν αὐτοῖς ὁ Ἰησοῦς, Ὁ καιρὸς ὁ ἐμὸς οὔπω πάρεστιν,[13] ὁ δὲ καιρὸς ὁ ὑμέτερος[14] πάντοτέ ἐστιν ἕτοιμος.[15] **7.** οὐ δύναται ὁ κόσμος <u>μισεῖν</u> ὑμᾶς, ἐμὲ δὲ μισεῖ, ὅτι ἐγὼ μαρτυρῶ περὶ αὐτοῦ ὅτι τὰ ἔργα αὐτοῦ πονηρά ἐστιν.

Parsing: ἤθελεν ....

εἶπον ....

μισεῖν ....

Translation: ....

....

....

....

....

....

....

....

....

....

....

....

---

[9]σκηνοπηγία, -ας, ἡ, *Feast of Tabernacles* (1).   [10]μεταβαίνω, *I go, pass over* (12).   [11]ἐντεῦθεν, *from here, from this* (10).   [12]κρυπτός, -ή, -όν, *hidden, secret* (17).   [13]πάρειμι, *I am present, have come* [Vocab 10].   [14]ὑμέτερος, -α, -ον, *your* (11).   [15]ἕτοιμος, -η, -ον, *ready, prepared* (17).

Reading 4 | John 7:8–13

8. ὑμεῖς <u>ἀνάβητε</u> εἰς τὴν ἑορτήν· ἐγὼ οὔπω ἀναβαίνω εἰς τὴν ἑορτὴν ταύτην, ὅτι ὁ ἐμὸς καιρὸς οὔπω πεπλήρωται. **9.** ταῦτα δὲ <u>εἰπὼν</u> αὐτὸς ἔμεινεν ἐν τῇ Γαλιλαίᾳ.

10. Ὡς δὲ ἀνέβησαν οἱ ἀδελφοὶ αὐτοῦ εἰς τὴν ἑορτήν, τότε καὶ αὐτὸς ἀνέβη, οὐ φανερῶς[16] ἀλλὰ ὡς ἐν κρυπτῷ.[17] **11.** οἱ οὖν Ἰουδαῖοι ἐζήτουν αὐτὸν ἐν τῇ ἑορτῇ καὶ ἔλεγον, Ποῦ ἐστιν ἐκεῖνος;

12. καὶ γογγυσμὸς[18] περὶ αὐτοῦ ἦν πολὺς ἐν τοῖς ὄχλοις· οἱ μὲν ἔλεγον ὅτι Ἀγαθός ἐστιν, ἄλλοι δὲ ἔλεγον, Οὔ, ἀλλὰ <u>πλανᾷ</u> τὸν ὄχλον. **13.** οὐδεὶς μέντοι[19] παρρησίᾳ ἐλάλει περὶ αὐτοῦ διὰ τὸν φόβον τῶν Ἰουδαίων.

Parsing: ἀνάβητε _____

εἰπὼν _____

πλανᾷ _____

Translation: _____

_____

_____

_____

_____

_____

_____

_____

_____

_____

_____

_____

[16]φανερῶς, *openly, clearly, plainly* (3).   [17]See verse 4.   [18]γογγυσμός, -οῦ, ὁ, *complaint, secret talk, whispering* (4).   [19]μέντοι, *really, truly, though, yet, however* (8).

Reading 5 | John 7:14–19

14. Ἤδη δὲ τῆς ἑορτῆς μεσούσης[20] ἀνέβη Ἰησοῦς εἰς τὸ ἱερὸν καὶ ἐδίδασκεν.

15. ἐθαύμαζον οὖν οἱ Ἰουδαῖοι λέγοντες, Πῶς οὗτος γράμματα[21] οἶδεν μὴ <u>μεμαθηκώς</u>;

16. ἀπεκρίθη οὖν αὐτοῖς ὁ Ἰησοῦς καὶ εἶπεν, Ἡ ἐμὴ διδαχὴ οὐκ ἔστιν ἐμὴ ἀλλὰ τοῦ πέμψαντός με· **17.** ἐάν τις θέλῃ τὸ θέλημα αὐτοῦ ποιεῖν, γνώσεται περὶ τῆς διδαχῆς πότερον[22] ἐκ τοῦ θεοῦ ἐστιν ἢ ἐγὼ ἀπ' ἐμαυτοῦ λαλῶ. **18.** ὁ ἀφ' ἑαυτοῦ λαλῶν τὴν δόξαν τὴν ἰδίαν <u>ζητεῖ</u>· ὁ δὲ ζητῶν τὴν δόξαν τοῦ πέμψαντος αὐτόν, οὗτος ἀληθής ἐστιν καὶ ἀδικία ἐν αὐτῷ οὐκ ἔστιν. **19.** οὐ Μωϋσῆς <u>δέδωκεν</u> ὑμῖν τὸν νόμον; καὶ οὐδεὶς ἐξ ὑμῶν ποιεῖ τὸν νόμον. τί με ζητεῖτε ἀποκτεῖναι;

Parsing: μεμαθηκώς _____

            ζητεῖ _____

            δέδωκεν _____

Translation: _____

_____

_____

_____

_____

_____

_____

_____

_____

_____

_____

_____

_____

_____

_____

---

[20]μεσόω, *I am in the middle, half over* (1).   [21]γράμμα, -ατος, τό, *letter (of the alphabet), book, document* (14).
[22]πότερον, *whether* (1).

Reading 6 | John 7:20–24

20. ἀπεκρίθη ὁ ὄχλος, Δαιμόνιον ἔχεις· τίς σε ζητεῖ ἀποκτεῖναι;

21. ἀπεκρίθη Ἰησοῦς καὶ εἶπεν αὐτοῖς, Ἓν ἔργον ἐποίησα καὶ πάντες θαυμάζετε. **22.** διὰ τοῦτο Μωϋσῆς δέδωκεν ὑμῖν τὴν περιτομήν—οὐχ ὅτι ἐκ τοῦ Μωϋσέως ἐστὶν ἀλλ᾽ ἐκ τῶν πατέρων—καὶ ἐν σαββάτῳ περιτέμνετε[23] ἄνθρωπον. **23.** εἰ περιτομὴν λαμβάνει ἄνθρωπος ἐν σαββάτῳ ἵνα μὴ <u>λυθῇ</u> ὁ νόμος Μωϋσέως, ἐμοὶ χολᾶτε[24] ὅτι ὅλον ἄνθρωπον ὑγιῆ[25] <u>ἐποίησα</u> ἐν σαββάτῳ; **24.** μὴ κρίνετε κατ᾽ ὄψιν,[26] ἀλλὰ τὴν <u>δικαίαν</u> κρίσιν κρίνετε.

Parsing: λυθῇ   _____

                ἐποίησα   _____

                δικαίαν   _____

Translation: _____

_____

_____

_____

_____

_____

_____

_____

_____

_____

_____

_____

_____

_____

---

[23]περιτέμνω, *I circumcise* (17).   [24]χολάω, *I am angry* (1).   [25]ὑγιής, -ές, *sound, healthy* (11).
[26]ὄψις, -εως, ἡ, *outward appearance* (3).

Vocabulary

Friends	Memory Aids
ἀδικία, -ας, ἡ, *unrighteousness, wrongdoing* (25).	(ἀ) + δίκαιος—righteousness.
Αἴγυπτος, -ου, ἡ, *Egypt* (25).	Just like it sounds.
ἀκοή, -ῆς, ἡ, *hearing, report* (24).	ἀκούω—I hear.
ἀναβλέπω, *I look up, receive sight* (25).	*Up*(ward) (ἀνά) *I look* (βλέπω).
ἀσθένεια, -ας, ἡ, *weakness, sickness* (24).	ἀσθενέω—I am weak.
ἀστήρ,-έρος, ὁ, *star* (24).	Asteroid.
γνωρίζω, *I make known, reveal* (25).	γινώσκω—I know.
δέκα, *ten* (25).	Decade—**ten** years.
δένδρον, -ου, τό, *tree* (25).	Dendrite—the branched end of a nerve cell.
δουλεύω, *I serve, obey* (25).	δοῦλος—slave.
Ἕλλην, -ηνος, ὁ, *Greek, Gentile, pagan* (25).	Hellenic.
ἐπιστολή, -ῆς, ἡ, *letter* (24).	Epistle.
λευκός, -ή, -όν, *white* (25).	Leukocyte—a **white** blood cell.
μήποτε, *never, lest* (25).	not (μή) ever (ποτέ).
πνευματικός, -ή, -όν, *spiritual* (26).	πνεῦμα—spirit.
πορνεία, -ας, ἡ, *fornication* (25).	Pornography.
φιλέω, *I love, kiss* (25).	φίλος—beloved, loving; friend.
Cousins	
ἀναιρέω, *I take away, kill* (24).	up(ward) (ἀνά) *I take* (αἴρω).
καταλείπω, *I leave behind, abandon* (24).	λοιπός—remaining.
μανθάνω, *I learn, find out* (25).	μαθητής—disciple.
Strangers	
γέ, *indeed, even* (25).	A gecko? *Indeed!*
ἑορτή, -ῆς, ἡ, *festival, feast* (26).	
κελεύω, *I command, order* (26).	I *ordered* Kahlua.
νεφέλη, -ης, ἡ, *cloud* (25).	Nepheliad—a cloud-nymph.
ὁμολογέω, *I confess, profess* (26).	I speak (λέγω) the same (ὅμοιος).
οὔπω, *not yet* (26).	
στρατιώτης, οῦ, ὁ, *soldier* (26).	A *soldier* relies on strategy.
συνίημι, *I understand, comprehend* (26).	
φρονέω, *I think, ponder* (26).	I frown when *I think* too hard.

Week Ten

John 8:12–45

[Reading 1 | John 8:12–16]

12. Πάλιν οὖν αὐτοῖς <u>ἐλάλησεν</u> ὁ Ἰησοῦς λέγων, Ἐγώ εἰμι τὸ φῶς τοῦ κόσμου· ὁ ἀκολουθῶν ἐμοὶ οὐ μὴ <u>περιπατήσῃ</u> ἐν τῇ σκοτίᾳ, ἀλλ᾽ ἕξει τὸ φῶς τῆς ζωῆς.

13. εἶπον οὖν αὐτῷ οἱ Φαρισαῖοι, Σὺ περὶ σεαυτοῦ μαρτυρεῖς· ἡ μαρτυρία σου οὐκ ἔστιν ἀληθής.

14. ἀπεκρίθη Ἰησοῦς καὶ εἶπεν αὐτοῖς, Κἂν[1] ἐγὼ μαρτυρῶ περὶ ἐμαυτοῦ, ἀληθής ἐστιν ἡ μαρτυρία μου, ὅτι οἶδα πόθεν ἦλθον καὶ ποῦ ὑπάγω· ὑμεῖς δὲ οὐκ οἴδατε πόθεν ἔρχομαι ἢ ποῦ ὑπάγω. **15.** ὑμεῖς κατὰ τὴν σάρκα κρίνετε, ἐγὼ οὐ κρίνω οὐδένα. **16.** καὶ ἐὰν κρίνω δὲ ἐγώ, ἡ κρίσις ἡ ἐμὴ <u>ἀληθινή</u> ἐστιν, ὅτι μόνος οὐκ εἰμί, ἀλλ᾽ ἐγὼ καὶ ὁ πέμψας με πατήρ.

Parsing: ἐλάλησεν _____

                 περιπατήσῃ _____

                 ἀληθινή _____

Translation: _____

_____

_____

_____

_____

_____

_____

_____

_____

_____

---

[1] κἄν, *and if, even if* (17).

Reading 2 | John 8:17–21

17. καὶ ἐν τῷ νόμῳ δὲ τῷ ὑμετέρῳ[2] <u>γέγραπται</u> ὅτι δύο ἀνθρώπων ἡ μαρτυρία ἀληθής ἐστιν. **18.** ἐγώ εἰμι ὁ μαρτυρῶν περὶ ἐμαυτοῦ καὶ μαρτυρεῖ περὶ ἐμοῦ ὁ πέμψας με πατήρ.

19. ἔλεγον οὖν αὐτῷ, Ποῦ ἐστιν ὁ πατήρ σου; ἀπεκρίθη Ἰησοῦς, Οὔτε ἐμὲ οἴδατε οὔτε τὸν πατέρα μου· εἰ ἐμὲ ᾔδειτε,[3] καὶ τὸν πατέρα μου ἂν[4] ᾔδειτε. **20.** Ταῦτα τὰ ῥήματα ἐλάλησεν ἐν τῷ γαζοφυλακίῳ[5] διδάσκων ἐν τῷ ἱερῷ· καὶ οὐδεὶς ἐπίασεν[6] αὐτόν, ὅτι οὔπω ἐληλύθει[7] ἡ ὥρα αὐτοῦ.

21. Εἶπεν οὖν πάλιν αὐτοῖς, Ἐγὼ ὑπάγω καὶ <u>ζητήσετέ</u> με, καὶ ἐν τῇ ἁμαρτίᾳ ὑμῶν <u>ἀποθανεῖσθε</u>· ὅπου ἐγὼ ὑπάγω ὑμεῖς οὐ δύνασθε ἐλθεῖν.

Parsing: γέγραπται   _____

               ζητήσετε   _____

               ἀποθανεῖσθε _____

Translation: _____

_____

_____

_____

_____

_____

_____

_____

_____

_____

_____

_____

_____

_____

[2]ὑμέτερος, -α, -ον, *your* (11).   [3]Here again is a pluperfect form of οἶδα. Translate it as *you knew.*   [4]What is this untranslatable particle signifying in this sentence?   [5]γαζοφυλάκιον, -ου, τό, *treasury, treasure room* (5). [6]πιάζω, *I seize, grasp, arrest* (12).   [7]This is the pluperfect form of ἔρχομαι. Translate it as *it had come.*

| Reading 3 | John 8:22–27 |

22. ἔλεγον οὖν οἱ Ἰουδαῖοι, Μήτι[8] <u>ἀποκτενεῖ</u> ἑαυτόν, ὅτι λέγει, Ὅπου ἐγὼ ὑπάγω ὑμεῖς οὐ δύνασθε ἐλθεῖν;

23. καὶ ἔλεγεν αὐτοῖς, Ὑμεῖς ἐκ τῶν κάτω[9] ἐστέ, ἐγὼ ἐκ τῶν ἄνω[10] εἰμί· ὑμεῖς ἐκ τούτου τοῦ κόσμου ἐστέ, ἐγὼ οὐκ εἰμὶ ἐκ τοῦ κόσμου τούτου.

24. εἶπον οὖν ὑμῖν ὅτι ἀποθανεῖσθε ἐν ταῖς ἁμαρτίαις ὑμῶν· ἐὰν γὰρ μὴ πιστεύσητε ὅτι ἐγώ εἰμι, ἀποθανεῖσθε ἐν ταῖς <u>ἁμαρτίαις</u> ὑμῶν.

25. ἔλεγον οὖν αὐτῷ, Σὺ τίς εἶ; εἶπεν αὐτοῖς ὁ Ἰησοῦς, Τὴν ἀρχὴν ὅ τι καὶ λαλῶ ὑμῖν;[11]

26. πολλὰ ἔχω περὶ ὑμῶν λαλεῖν καὶ κρίνειν· ἀλλ' ὁ πέμψας με ἀληθής ἐστιν, κἀγὼ ἃ ἤκουσα παρ' αὐτοῦ ταῦτα λαλῶ εἰς τὸν κόσμον.

27. οὐκ <u>ἔγνωσαν</u> ὅτι τὸν πατέρα αὐτοῖς ἔλεγεν.

Parsing: ἀποκτενεῖ _____

            ἁμαρτίαις _____

            ἔγνωσαν _____

Translation: _____

_____

_____

_____

_____

_____

_____

_____

_____

_____

_____

_____

_____

---

[8]μήτι, *an untranslatable particle used in questions which expect a negative answer* (17).   [9]κάτω, *below, down* (9).
[10]ἄνω, *above, up* (9).   [11]This is a notoriously difficult verse to translate. We have followed BAGD s.v. ἀρχή, 1.b—*How is it that I even speak to you at all?*

| Reading 4 | John 8:28–33 |

28. εἶπεν οὖν ὁ Ἰησοῦς, Ὅταν ὑψώσητε[12] τὸν υἱὸν τοῦ ἀνθρώπου, τότε γνώσεσθε ὅτι ἐγώ εἰμι, καὶ ἀπ᾽ <u>ἐμαυτοῦ</u> ποιῶ οὐδέν, ἀλλὰ καθὼς ἐδίδαξέν με ὁ πατὴρ ταῦτα λαλῶ. **29.** καὶ ὁ πέμψας με μετ᾽ ἐμοῦ ἐστιν· οὐκ <u>ἀφῆκέν</u> με μόνον, ὅτι ἐγὼ τὰ ἀρεστὰ[13] αὐτῷ ποιῶ πάντοτε. **30.** Ταῦτα αὐτοῦ λαλοῦντος πολλοὶ ἐπίστευσαν εἰς αὐτόν.

31. Ἔλεγεν οὖν ὁ Ἰησοῦς πρὸς τοὺς πεπιστευκότας αὐτῷ Ἰουδαίους, Ἐὰν ὑμεῖς μείνητε ἐν τῷ λόγῳ τῷ ἐμῷ, ἀληθῶς[14] μαθηταί μού ἐστε, **32.** καὶ γνώσεσθε τὴν ἀλήθειαν, καὶ ἡ ἀλήθεια ἐλευθερώσει[15] ὑμᾶς.

33. ἀπεκρίθησαν πρὸς αὐτόν, Σπέρμα Ἀβραάμ <u>ἐσμεν</u> καὶ οὐδενὶ δεδουλεύκαμεν πώποτε·[16] πῶς σὺ λέγεις ὅτι Ἐλεύθεροι γενήσεσθε;

Parsing: ἐμαυτοῦ _____

ἀφῆκέν _____

ἐσμεν _____

Translation:

_____

_____

_____

_____

_____

_____

_____

_____

_____

_____

_____

_____

---

[12]ὑψόω, *I lift up, exalt* [Vocab. 12].   [13]ἀρεστός, -ή, -όν, *pleasing* (4).   [14]ἀληθῶς, *truly* (18).
[15]ἐλευθερόω, *I free, set free* (7).   [16]πώποτε, *ever, at any time* (6).

Reading 5 | John 8:34–40

34. ἀπεκρίθη αὐτοῖς ὁ Ἰησοῦς, Ἀμὴν ἀμὴν λέγω ὑμῖν ὅτι πᾶς ὁ <u>ποιῶν</u> τὴν ἁμαρτίαν δοῦλός ἐστιν τῆς ἁμαρτίας. **35.** ὁ δὲ δοῦλος οὐ μένει ἐν τῇ οἰκίᾳ εἰς τὸν αἰῶνα· ὁ υἱὸς μένει εἰς τὸν αἰῶνα. **36.** ἐὰν οὖν ὁ υἱὸς ὑμᾶς ἐλευθερώσῃ,[17] ὄντως[18] ἐλεύθεροι ἔσεσθε. **37.** οἶδα ὅτι σπέρμα Ἀβραάμ ἐστε· ἀλλὰ ζητεῖτέ με ἀποκτεῖναι, ὅτι ὁ λόγος ὁ ἐμὸς οὐ χωρεῖ[19] ἐν ὑμῖν. **38.** ἃ ἐγὼ <u>ἑώρακα</u> παρὰ τῷ πατρὶ λαλῶ· καὶ ὑμεῖς οὖν ἃ ἠκούσατε παρὰ τοῦ πατρὸς ποιεῖτε.

39. Ἀπεκρίθησαν καὶ εἶπαν αὐτῷ, Ὁ πατὴρ ἡμῶν Ἀβραάμ ἐστιν. λέγει αὐτοῖς ὁ Ἰησοῦς, Εἰ <u>τέκνα</u> τοῦ Ἀβραάμ ἦτε, τὰ ἔργα τοῦ Ἀβραὰμ ἐποιεῖτε· **40.** νῦν δὲ ζητεῖτέ με ἀποκτεῖναι, ἄνθρωπον ὃς τὴν ἀλήθειαν ὑμῖν λελάληκα ἣν ἤκουσα παρὰ τοῦ θεοῦ· τοῦτο Ἀβραὰμ οὐκ ἐποίησεν.

Parsing: ποιῶν _____

ἑώρακα _____

τέκνα _____

Translation:

_____

_____

_____

_____

_____

_____

_____

_____

_____

_____

_____

_____

_____

---

[17]See verse 32.   [18]ὄντως, _really, truly_ (10).   [19]χωρέω, _I make progress, hold, contain_ (10).

Reading 6 | John 8:41–45

41. ὑμεῖς ποιεῖτε τὰ ἔργα τοῦ πατρὸς ὑμῶν. εἶπαν αὐτῷ, Ἡμεῖς ἐκ πορνείας οὐ

<u>γεγεννήμεθα</u>· ἕνα πατέρα ἔχομεν τὸν θεόν.

42. εἶπεν αὐτοῖς ὁ Ἰησοῦς, Εἰ ὁ θεὸς πατὴρ ὑμῶν ἦν, ἠγαπᾶτε ἂν ἐμέ, ἐγὼ γὰρ ἐκ τοῦ

θεοῦ ἐξῆλθον καὶ ἥκω· οὐδὲ γὰρ ἀπ᾽ ἐμαυτοῦ <u>ἐλήλυθα</u>, ἀλλ᾽ ἐκεῖνός με ἀπέστειλεν. **43.** διὰ τί

τὴν λαλιὰν[20] τὴν ἐμὴν οὐ γινώσκετε; ὅτι οὐ δύνασθε ἀκούειν τὸν λόγον τὸν ἐμόν. **44.** ὑμεῖς ἐκ

τοῦ πατρὸς τοῦ διαβόλου ἐστὲ καὶ τὰς ἐπιθυμίας τοῦ πατρὸς ὑμῶν θέλετε ποιεῖν. ἐκεῖνος

ἀνθρωποκτόνος[21] ἦν ἀπ᾽ ἀρχῆς καὶ ἐν τῇ ἀληθείᾳ οὐκ ἔστηκεν,[22] ὅτι οὐκ ἔστιν ἀλήθεια ἐν

αὐτῷ. ὅταν <u>λαλῇ</u> τὸ ψεῦδος,[23] ἐκ τῶν ἰδίων λαλεῖ, ὅτι ψεύστης[24] ἐστὶν καὶ ὁ πατὴρ αὐτοῦ.

45. ἐγὼ δὲ ὅτι τὴν ἀλήθειαν λέγω, οὐ πιστεύετέ μοι.

Parsing: γεγεννήμεθα _____

ἐλήλυθα _____

λαλῇ _____

Translation: _____

_____

_____

_____

_____

_____

_____

_____

_____

_____

_____

_____

_____

_____

---

[20]λαλιά, -ᾶς, ἡ, *speech, way of speaking* (3).   [21]ἀνθρωποκτόνος, -ου, ὁ, *murderer* (3).   [22]στήκω, *I stand, stand firm* (10).   [23]ψεῦδος, -ους, τό, *lie, falsehood* (10).   [24]ψεύστης, -ου, ὁ, *liar* (10).

Vocabulary

Friends	Memory Aids
ἀνάγω, *I lead up, bring up, put to sea* (23).	I *lead* (ἄγω) *up* (ἀνά).
ἄπιστος, -ον, *unbelieving, faithless* (23).	(ἀ) + πιστός—faithful.
εἰκών, -όνος, ἡ, *image, likeness* (23).	Icon.
ζῷον, -ου, τό, *living thing, animal* (23).	Zoology.
θυσιαστήριον, -ου, τό, *altar* (23).	θυσία—sacrifice (made at an *altar*).
νέος, -α, -ον, *new, fresh, young* (23).	Neo—*new*.
παῖς, παιδός, ὁ, ἡ, *boy, girl, child, servant* (24).	παιδίον—*child*.
σωτήρ, -ῆρος, ὁ, *Savior, rescuer* (24).	σωτηρία—salvation.
τελειόω, *I fulfill, make perfect* (23).	τελέω—I finish, complete.
Τιμόθεος, -ου, ὁ, *Timothy* (24).	Just like it sounds.
χαρίζομαι, *I give freely, forgive* (23).	χάρις is a gift *given freely*.

Cousins	
διότι, *because, therefore* (23).	διά—*because* of.
μιμνήσκομαι, *I remember* (23).	A mnemonic is a memory aid.
νοῦς, νοός, ὁ, *mind, intellect* (24).	μετανοέω—I change my *mind* (repent).
πάρειμι, *I am present, have come* (24).	*I am* (εἰμί) with/*present* (παρά).
παρουσία, -ας, ἡ, *presence, coming* (24).	Related to πάρειμι.

Strangers	
ἀμπελών, -ῶνος, ὁ, *vineyard* (23).	There are ample grapes in the *vineyard*.
αὐξάνω, *I grow, increase* (23).	
ἐλεύθερος, -α, -ον, *free, independent* (23).	I elude capture.
κατηγορέω, *I accuse* (23).	
κεῖμαι, *I lie, am laid* (24).	
κοπιάω, *I work hard, labor* (23).	*Hard work* yields a copious return.
κωλύω, *I forbid, hinder* (23).	I *forbid* a collusion.
οὗ, *where, to which* (24).	
πεινάω, *I hunger, am hungry* (23).	I pine for food (*hunger*).
πέραν, *on the other side, across* (23).	Let us perambulate to the *other side*.
περιβάλλω, *I put on, clothe* (23).	Periblem—something *put on*.
πίμπλημι, *I fill, fulfill* (24).	A pimple is a *filled* pustule.
προσέχω, *I pay attention to, care for* (24).	A prosecutor *pays attention* to the testimony.
σκεῦος, -ους, τό, *object, vessel* (23).	The *vessel* was skewed.
χιλιάς, -άδος, ἡ, *thousand* (23).	Chiliasm—doctrine of Christ's *thousand*-year earthly reign.

Week Eleven

Mark 13:3–37

Reading 1 | Mark 13:3–8

3. Καὶ <u>καθημένου</u> αὐτοῦ εἰς τὸ Ὄρος τῶν Ἐλαιῶν[1] κατέναντι[2] τοῦ ἱεροῦ ἐπηρώτα αὐτὸν κατ᾽ ἰδίαν[3] Πέτρος καὶ Ἰάκωβος καὶ Ἰωάννης καὶ Ἀνδρέας, **4.** Εἰπὸν ἡμῖν πότε ταῦτα ἔσται καὶ τί τὸ σημεῖον ὅταν <u>μέλλῃ</u> ταῦτα συντελεῖσθαι[4] πάντα.

5. ὁ δὲ Ἰησοῦς ἤρξατο λέγειν αὐτοῖς, Βλέπετε μή τις ὑμᾶς πλανήσῃ· **6.** πολλοὶ ἐλεύσονται ἐπὶ τῷ ὀνόματί μου λέγοντες ὅτι Ἐγώ εἰμι, καὶ πολλοὺς πλανήσουσιν. **7.** ὅταν δὲ ἀκούσητε πολέμους[5] καὶ ἀκοὰς πολέμων, μὴ θροεῖσθε·[6] δεῖ γενέσθαι, ἀλλ᾽ οὔπω τὸ τέλος. **8.** ἐγερθήσεται γὰρ ἔθνος ἐπ᾽ ἔθνος καὶ βασιλεία ἐπὶ βασιλείαν, <u>ἔσονται</u> σεισμοὶ[7] κατὰ[8] τόπους, ἔσονται λιμοί·[9] ἀρχὴ ὠδίνων[10] ταῦτα.

Parsing: καθημένου _____

μέλλῃ _____

ἔσονται _____

Translation: _____

_____

_____

_____

_____

_____

_____

_____

_____

---

[1]ἐλαία, -ας, ἡ, *olive, olive tree* (13).   [2]κατέναντι, *opposite, in sight of* (8).   [3]Translate κατ᾽ ἰδίαν as *privately* (BAGD s.v. ἴδιος, 4).   [4]συντελέω, *I complete, come to an end* (6).   [5]πόλεμος, -ου, ὁ, *war, battle* (18). [6]θροέω, *I am disturbed, frightened* (3). This verb is always passive in the New Testament.   [7]σεισμός, -οῦ, ὁ, *earthquake, shaking* (14).   [8]Here, as in verse 3, none of the definitions you have memorized for κατά seem to fit. In this case κατά is used to emphasize a distributive idea. There will be earthquakes distributed throughout various places. Translate it as *in* (BAGD s.v. κατά, II.1.d).   [9]λιμός, -οῦ, ὁ, ἡ, *hunger, famine* (12).   [10]ὠδίν, -ῖνος, ἡ, *birth pains, suffering* (4).

Reading 2 | Mark 13:9–13

9. βλέπετε δὲ ὑμεῖς ἑαυτούς· παραδώσουσιν ὑμᾶς εἰς συνέδρια καὶ εἰς <u>συναγωγὰς</u>

δαρήσεσθε[11] καὶ ἐπὶ ἡγεμόνων[12] καὶ βασιλέων <u>σταθήσεσθε</u> ἕνεκεν ἐμοῦ εἰς μαρτύριον[13]

αὐτοῖς. **10.** καὶ εἰς πάντα τὰ ἔθνη πρῶτον δεῖ κηρυχθῆναι τὸ εὐαγγέλιον. **11.** καὶ ὅταν ἄγωσιν

ὑμᾶς παραδιδόντες, μὴ προμεριμνᾶτε[14] τί λαλήσητε, ἀλλ᾽ ὃ ἐὰν <u>δοθῇ</u> ὑμῖν ἐν ἐκείνῃ τῇ ὥρᾳ

τοῦτο λαλεῖτε, οὐ γάρ ἐστε ὑμεῖς οἱ λαλοῦντες ἀλλὰ τὸ πνεῦμα τὸ ἅγιον.

12. καὶ παραδώσει ἀδελφὸς ἀδελφὸν εἰς θάνατον καὶ πατὴρ τέκνον, καὶ

ἐπαναστήσονται[15] τέκνα ἐπὶ γονεῖς[16] καὶ θανατώσουσιν αὐτούς· **13.** καὶ ἔσεσθε μισούμενοι

ὑπὸ πάντων διὰ τὸ ὄνομά μου. ὁ δὲ ὑπομείνας[17] εἰς τέλος οὗτος σωθήσεται.

Parsing: συναγωγὰς _____

              σταθήσεσθε _____

              δοθῇ _____

Translation:

---

[11]δέρω, *I skin, beat* (15).   [12]ἡγεμών, -όνος, ὁ, *prince, governor* [Vocab. 12].   [13]μαρτύριον, -ου, τό, *testimony, proof* (19).   [14]προμεριμνάω, *I am anxious beforehand, worry beforehand* (1).   [15]ἐπανίστημι, *I set up, rise in rebellion* (2).   [16]γονεύς, -έως, ὁ, *parent, parents* [Vocab. 12].   [17]ὑπομένω, *I endure, remain, hold out* (17).

Reading 3 | Mark 13:14–19

14. Ὅταν δὲ ἴδητε τὸ βδέλυγμα[18] τῆς ἐρημώσεως[19] ἑστηκότα ὅπου οὐ δεῖ, ὁ ἀναγινώσκων νοείτω,[20] τότε οἱ ἐν τῇ Ἰουδαίᾳ φευγέτωσαν εἰς τὰ ὄρη, **15.** ὁ δὲ ἐπὶ τοῦ δώματος[21] μὴ καταβάτω μηδὲ εἰσελθάτω ἆραί τι ἐκ τῆς οἰκίας αὐτοῦ, **16.** καὶ ὁ εἰς τὸν ἀγρὸν μὴ ἐπιστρεψάτω εἰς τὰ ὀπίσω ἆραι τὸ ἱμάτιον αὐτοῦ. **17.** οὐαὶ δὲ ταῖς ἐν γαστρὶ[22] ἐχούσαις καὶ ταῖς θηλαζούσαις[23] ἐν ἐκείναις ταῖς ἡμέραις. **18.** προσεύχεσθε δὲ ἵνα μὴ γένηται χειμῶνος·[24] **19.** ἔσονται γὰρ αἱ ἡμέραι ἐκεῖναι θλῖψις οἵα[25] οὐ γέγονεν τοιαύτη ἀπ' ἀρχῆς κτίσεως[26] ἣν ἔκτισεν[27] ὁ θεὸς ἕως τοῦ νῦν καὶ οὐ μὴ γένηται.

Parsing: ἆραί _____

ἐκεῖναι _____

γένηται _____

Translation: _____

_____

_____

_____

_____

_____

_____

_____

_____

_____

_____

_____

_____

_____

_____

_____

_____

_____

[18]βδέλυγμα, -ατος, τό, *abomination, detestable thing* (6).   [19]ἐρήμωσις, -εως, ἡ, *devastation, desolation* (3). [20]νοέω, *I perceive, understand* (14).   [21]δῶμα, -ατος, τό, *roof, housetop* (7).   [22]γαστήρ, -τρός, ἡ, *belly, womb* (9).   [23]θηλάζω, I nurse, suck (5).   [24]χειμών, -ῶνος, ὁ, *winter, rainy and stormy weather, bad weather* (6). [25]οἷος, -α, -ον, *of what sort, such as* (14).   [26]κτίσις, -εως, ἡ, *creation, world* (19).   [27]κτίζω, *I create, make* (15).

Reading 4 | Mark 13:20–25

20. καὶ εἰ μὴ ἐκολόβωσεν[28] κύριος τὰς ἡμέρας, οὐκ ἂν <u>ἐσώθη</u> πᾶσα σάρξ. ἀλλὰ διὰ τοὺς ἐκλεκτοὺς οὓς <u>ἐξελέξατο</u> ἐκολόβωσεν τὰς ἡμέρας. **21.** καὶ τότε ἐάν τις ὑμῖν εἴπῃ, Ἴδε ὧδε ὁ Χριστός, Ἴδε ἐκεῖ, μὴ πιστεύετε· **22.** <u>ἐγερθήσονται</u> γὰρ ψευδόχριστοι[29] καὶ ψευδοπροφῆται[30] καὶ δώσουσιν σημεῖα καὶ τέρατα[31] πρὸς τὸ ἀποπλανᾶν,[32] εἰ δυνατόν, τοὺς ἐκλεκτούς. **23.** ὑμεῖς δὲ βλέπετε· προείρηκα[33] ὑμῖν πάντα.

24. Ἀλλὰ ἐν ἐκείναις ταῖς ἡμέραις μετὰ τὴν θλῖψιν ἐκείνην ὁ ἥλιος σκοτισθήσεται,[34] καὶ ἡ σελήνη[35] οὐ δώσει τὸ φέγγος[36] αὐτῆς,

25. καὶ οἱ ἀστέρες ἔσονται ἐκ τοῦ οὐρανοῦ πίπτοντες, καὶ αἱ δυνάμεις αἱ ἐν τοῖς οὐρανοῖς σαλευθήσονται.[37]

Parsing: ἐσώθη _____

ἐξελέξατο _____

ἐγερθήσονται _____

Translation: _____

_____

_____

_____

_____

_____

_____

_____

_____

_____

_____

_____

_____

---

[28]κολοβόω, *I curtail, shorten* (4).   [29]ψευδόχριστος, -ου, ὁ, *false Christ, false Messiah* (2). [30]ψευδοπροφήτης, ου, ὁ, *false prophet* (11).   [31]τέρας, -ατος, τό, *portent, omen* (16).   [32]ἀποπλανάω, *I mislead, deceive* (2).   [33]προλέγω, *I tell beforehand* (15).   [34]σκοτίζω, *I am or become dark* (5). Always passive in the NT.   [35]σελήνη, -ης, ἡ, *moon* (9).   [36]φέγγος, -ους, τό, *light, radiance* (2).   [37]σαλεύω, *I shake, cause to move* (15).

Reading 5 | Mark 13:26–31

26. καὶ τότε <u>ὄψονται</u> τὸν υἱὸν τοῦ ἀνθρώπου ἐρχόμενον ἐν νεφέλαις μετὰ δυνάμεως πολλῆς καὶ δόξης. **27.** καὶ τότε ἀποστελεῖ τοὺς ἀγγέλους καὶ ἐπισυνάξει[38] τοὺς ἐκλεκτοὺς αὐτοῦ ἐκ τῶν τεσσάρων ἀνέμων ἀπ' ἄκρου[39] γῆς ἕως[40] ἄκρου οὐρανοῦ.

28. Ἀπὸ δὲ τῆς συκῆς[41] <u>μάθετε</u> τὴν παραβολήν· ὅταν ἤδη ὁ κλάδος[42] αὐτῆς ἁπαλὸς[43] γένηται καὶ ἐκφύῃ[44] τὰ φύλλα,[45] γινώσκετε ὅτι ἐγγὺς τὸ θέρος[46] ἐστίν· **29.** οὕτως καὶ ὑμεῖς, ὅταν ἴδητε ταῦτα γινόμενα, γινώσκετε ὅτι ἐγγύς ἐστιν ἐπὶ <u>θύραις</u>. **30.** ἀμὴν λέγω ὑμῖν ὅτι οὐ μὴ παρέλθῃ ἡ γενεὰ αὕτη μέχρις[47] οὗ ταῦτα πάντα γένηται. **31.** ὁ οὐρανὸς καὶ ἡ γῆ παρελεύσονται, οἱ δὲ λόγοι μου οὐ μὴ παρελεύσονται.

Parsing: ὄψονται _____

               μάθετε _____

               θύραις _____

Translation:

---

[38]ἐπισυνάγω, *I gather together* (8).   [39]ἄκρον, -ου, τό, *high point, top, extreme end* (6).   [40]When followed by a genitive of place, ἕως can be translated as *to* (BAGD, s.v. ἕως, II.2.a).   [41]συκῆ, -ῆς, ἡ, *fig tree* (16). [42]κλάδος, -ου, ὁ, *branch* (11).   [43]ἁπαλός, -ή, -όν, *tender* (2).   [44]ἐκφύω, *I put forth, generate* (2). [45]φύλλον, -ου, τό, *leaf* (6).   [46]θέρος, ους, τό, *summer* (3).   [47]μέχρι, *until* (17).

> **Reading 6** | **Mark 13:32–37**

32. Περὶ δὲ τῆς ἡμέρας ἐκείνης ἢ τῆς ὥρας οὐδεὶς οἶδεν, οὐδὲ οἱ ἄγγελοι ἐν οὐρανῷ οὐδὲ ὁ υἱός, εἰ μὴ ὁ πατήρ. **33.** βλέπετε, ἀγρυπνεῖτε·[48] οὐκ οἴδατε γὰρ πότε[49] ὁ καιρός ἐστιν. **34.** ὡς ἄνθρωπος ἀπόδημος[50] <u>ἀφεὶς</u> τὴν οἰκίαν αὐτοῦ καὶ <u>δοὺς</u> τοῖς δούλοις αὐτοῦ τὴν ἐξουσίαν, ἑκάστῳ τὸ ἔργον αὐτοῦ καὶ τῷ θυρωρῷ[51] ἐνετείλατο[52] ἵνα γρηγορῇ.

35. γρηγορεῖτε οὖν, οὐκ οἴδατε γὰρ πότε ὁ κύριος τῆς οἰκίας ἔρχεται, ἢ ὀψὲ[53] ἢ μεσονύκτιον[54] ἢ ἀλεκτοροφωνίας[55] ἢ πρωΐ,[56] **36.** μὴ ἐλθὼν ἐξαίφνης[57] <u>εὕρῃ</u> ὑμᾶς καθεύδοντας. **37.** ὃ δὲ ὑμῖν λέγω, πᾶσιν λέγω, γρηγορεῖτε.

Parsing: ἀφεὶς _____

δοὺς _____

εὕρῃ _____

Translation: _____

_____

_____

_____

_____

_____

_____

_____

_____

_____

_____

_____

_____

_____

---

[48]ἀγρυπνέω, *I am awake, guard* (4).   [49]πότε, *when* (19).   [50]ἀπόδημος, -ον, *absent* (1).   [51]θυρωρός, -οῦ, ὁ, ἡ, *doorkeeper* (4).   [52]ἐντέλλομαι, *I give orders, command* (15).   [53]ὀψέ, *late in the day, in the evening* (3). [54]μεσονύκτιον, -ου, τό, *midnight* (4).   [55]ἀλεκτοροφωνία, -ας, ἡ, *cock's crow, before dawn* (1).   [56]πρωΐ, *early in the morning, morning* (12).   [57]ἐξαίφνης, *suddenly, unexpectedly* (5).

Vocabulary

Friends	Memory Aids
ἀγνοέω, *I do not know, am ignorant* (22).	Agnostic.
βασιλεύω, *I am king, rule* (21).	Βασιλεύς—*king*.
διδασκαλία, -ας, ἡ, *teaching, instruction* (21).	διδάσκαλος—teacher.
ἐνεργέω, *I work, produce* (21).	ἔργον—work.
ἐφίστημι, *I stand by, appear* (21).	I *stand* (ἵστημι) *by* (ἐπί).
κἀκεῖνος, -η, -ο, *and that one* (22).	And (καί) that one (ἐκεῖνος).
Μακεδονία, -ας, ἡ, *Macedonia* (22).	Just like it sounds.
μετάνοια, -ας, ἡ, *repentance, conversion* (22).	Metanoia.
μηκέτι, *no longer* (22).	οὐκέτι—no longer.
πληγή, -ῆς, ἡ, *blow, plague* (22).	Just like it sounds.
πλοῦτος, ου, ὁ, τό, *wealth, riches* (22).	πλούσιος—rich, wealthy.
συνέδριον, -ου, τό, *Sanhedrin, council* (22).	Just like it sounds.
τεσσεράκοντα, *forty* (22).	τέσσαρες—four.
Cousins	
γρηγορέω, *I am awake, am watchful* (22).	ἐγείρω—I wake.
δοκιμάζω, *I examine, test, approve* (22).	I *test* by thinking (δοκέω).
ἐκλεκτός, -ή, -όν, *chosen, elect* (22).	Drop the first κ and you have *elect*.
ἐκλέγομαι, *I choose, select* (22).	Related to ἐκλεκτός.
εὐδοκέω, *I am well pleased, content* (21).	I think (δοκέω) *well* (εὖ).
Ἠσαΐας, -ου ὁ, *Isaiah* (22).	Similar to how it sounds; try rearranging the letters.
θεάομαι, *I see, look at* (22).	θεωρέω—I *look* at.
κατεργάζομαι, *I do, achieve* (22).	ἔργον—work, deed.
Strangers	
ἀντί, *instead of, for* (22).	Christ *instead of* the <u>anti</u>christ.
δέομαι, *I ask, beg, pray* (22).	
θερίζω, *I reap, harvest* (21).	
καθεύδω, *I sleep* (22).	
καθίστημι, *I bring, appoint* (21).	I set (ἵστημι) someone down (κατά).
κοιλία, -ας, ἡ, *belly, womb* (22).	The <u>col</u>on is <u>coil</u>ed in the *belly*.
λατρεύω, *I serve, worship* (21).	Latreutic—pertaining to *worship*.
πωλέω, *I sell, am sold* (22).	He *sells* insurance <u>poli</u>cies.

Week Twelve

John 5:1–38

Reading 1 | John 5:1–7

1. Μετὰ ταῦτα <u>ἦν</u> ἑορτὴ τῶν Ἰουδαίων, καὶ ἀνέβη Ἰησοῦς εἰς Ἱεροσόλυμα. **2.** ἔστιν δὲ ἐν τοῖς Ἱεροσολύμοις ἐπὶ τῇ προβατικῇ[1] κολυμβήθρα[2] ἡ ἐπιλεγομένη[3] Ἑβραϊστὶ[4] Βηθζαθά,[5] πέντε στοὰς[6] ἔχουσα. **3.** ἐν ταύταις κατέκειτο[7] πλῆθος τῶν ἀσθενούντων, τυφλῶν, χωλῶν,[8] ξηρῶν.[9] **5.** ἦν δὲ τις ἄνθρωπος ἐκεῖ τριάκοντα[10] καὶ ὀκτὼ[11] ἔτη ἔχων ἐν τῇ ἀσθενείᾳ αὐτοῦ· **6.** τοῦτον ἰδὼν ὁ Ἰησοῦς κατακείμενον καὶ <u>γνοὺς</u> ὅτι πολὺν ἤδη χρόνον ἔχει, λέγει αὐτῷ, Θέλεις ὑγιὴς[12] γενέσθαι;

7. ἀπεκρίθη αὐτῷ ὁ ἀσθενῶν, Κύριε, ἄνθρωπον οὐκ ἔχω ἵνα ὅταν ταραχθῇ[13] τὸ ὕδωρ <u>βάλῃ</u> με εἰς τὴν κολυμβήθραν· ἐν ᾧ δὲ ἔρχομαι ἐγὼ ἄλλος πρὸ ἐμοῦ καταβαίνει.

Parsing: ἦν   _____

                 γνοὺς _____

                 βάλῃ _____

Translation:

---

[1]προβατικός, ή, όν, *pertaining to sheep* (1). This refers to the gate placed in the north wall of Jerusalem (*BAGD,* s.v. προβατικός).   [2]κολυμβήθρα, ας, ἡ, *pool, swimming pool* (3).   [3]ἐπιλέγω, *I call, name* (2).   [4]Ἑβραϊστί, *in Hebrew or Aramaic* (7).   [5]βηθζαθά, ἡ, *Bethzatha* (1).   [6]στοά, ᾶς, ἡ, *colonnade, porch* (4).   [7]κατάκειμαι, *I recline, lie down* (12).   [8]χωλός, ή, όν, *lame, crippled* (14).   [9]ξηρός, ά, όν, *withered* (8).   [10]τριάκοντα, *thirty* (11).   [11]ὀκτώ, *eight* (8).   [12]ὑγιής, ές, *healthy, sound* (11).   [13]ταράσσω, *I stir up, disturb* (17).

Reading 2 | John 5:8–13

8. λέγει αὐτῷ ὁ Ἰησοῦς, Ἔγειρε <u>ἆρον</u> τὸν κράβαττόν[14] σου καὶ περιπάτει. **9.** καὶ εὐθέως ἐγένετο ὑγιὴς[15] ὁ ἄνθρωπος, καὶ ἦρεν τὸν κράβαττον αὐτοῦ καὶ περιεπάτει. Ἦν δὲ σάββατον ἐν ἐκείνῃ τῇ ἡμέρᾳ. **10.** ἔλεγον οὖν οἱ Ἰουδαῖοι τῷ <u>τεθεραπευμένῳ</u>, Σάββατόν ἐστιν, καὶ οὐκ ἔξεστιν σοι ἆραι τὸν κράβαττόν σου.

11. ὁ δὲ ἀπεκρίθη αὐτοῖς, Ὁ ποιήσας με ὑγιῆ ἐκεῖνός μοι εἶπεν, Ἆρον τὸν κράβαττόν σου καὶ περιπάτει.

12. ἠρώτησαν αὐτόν, Τίς ἐστιν ὁ ἄνθρωπος ὁ εἰπών σοι, Ἆρον καὶ περιπάτει;

13. ὁ δὲ <u>ἰαθεὶς</u> οὐκ ᾔδει[16] τίς ἐστιν, ὁ γὰρ Ἰησοῦς ἐξένευσεν[17] ὄχλου ὄντος ἐν τῷ τόπῳ.

Parsing: ἆρον _____

τεθεραπευμένῳ _____

ἰαθεὶς _____

Translation: _____

_____

_____

_____

_____

_____

_____

_____

_____

_____

_____

_____

_____

_____

_____

_____

---

[14]κράβαττος, ου, ὁ, _mattress, pallet_ (11).   [15]See verse 6.   [16]This is the pluperfect form of οἶδα. Translate it as _he knew_ (see _BBG,_ 232; Wallace, 586).   [17]ἐκνεύω, _I turn, withdraw_ (1).

Reading 3 | John 5:14–19

14. μετὰ ταῦτα εὑρίσκει αὐτὸν ὁ Ἰησοῦς ἐν τῷ ἱερῷ καὶ εἶπεν αὐτῷ, Ἴδε ὑγιὴς[18] γέγονας· μηκέτι <u>ἁμάρτανε</u>, ἵνα μὴ χεῖρόν[19] σοί τι γένηται. **15.** ἀπῆλθεν ὁ ἄνθρωπος καὶ ἀνήγγειλεν[20] τοῖς Ἰουδαίοις ὅτι Ἰησοῦς ἐστιν ὁ ποιήσας αὐτὸν ὑγιῆ.

16. καὶ διὰ τοῦτο ἐδίωκον οἱ Ἰουδαῖοι τὸν Ἰησοῦν, ὅτι ταῦτα ἐποίει ἐν σαββάτῳ. **17.** ὁ δὲ Ἰησοῦς <u>ἀπεκρίνατο</u> αὐτοῖς, Ὁ πατήρ μου ἕως ἄρτι ἐργάζεται, κἀγὼ ἐργάζομαι. **18.** διὰ τοῦτο οὖν μᾶλλον ἐζήτουν αὐτὸν οἱ Ἰουδαῖοι ἀποκτεῖναι, ὅτι οὐ μόνον <u>ἔλυεν</u> τὸ σάββατον ἀλλὰ καὶ πατέρα ἴδιον ἔλεγεν τὸν θεόν ἴσον[21] ἑαυτὸν ποιῶν τῷ θεῷ.

19. Ἀπεκρίνατο οὖν ὁ Ἰησοῦς καὶ ἔλεγεν αὐτοῖς, Ἀμὴν ἀμὴν λέγω ὑμῖν, οὐ δύναται ὁ υἱὸς ποιεῖν ἀφ' ἑαυτοῦ οὐδὲν ἐὰν μή τι βλέπῃ τὸν πατέρα ποιοῦντα· ἃ γὰρ ἂν ἐκεῖνος ποιῇ, ταῦτα καὶ ὁ υἱὸς ὁμοίως ποιεῖ.

Parsing: ἁμάρτανε _____

ἀπεκρίνατο _____

ἔλυεν _____

Translation:

_____

_____

_____

_____

_____

_____

_____

_____

_____

_____

_____

_____

---

[18]See verse 6.   [19]χείρων, ον, *worse, more severe* (11).   [20]ἀναγγέλλω, *I report, disclose, announce* (14).
[21]ἴσος, η, ον, *equal, same* (8).

Reading 4 | John 5:20–26

20. ὁ γὰρ πατὴρ φιλεῖ τὸν υἱὸν καὶ πάντα δείκνυσιν αὐτῷ ἃ αὐτὸς ποιεῖ, καὶ μείζονα τούτων <u>δείξει</u> αὐτῷ ἔργα, ἵνα ὑμεῖς θαυμάζητε. **21.** ὥσπερ γὰρ ὁ πατὴρ ἐγείρει τοὺς νεκροὺς καὶ ζῳοποιεῖ,[22] οὕτως καὶ ὁ υἱὸς οὓς θέλει ζῳοποιεῖ. **22.** οὐδὲ γὰρ ὁ πατὴρ κρίνει οὐδένα, ἀλλὰ τὴν κρίσιν πᾶσαν δέδωκεν τῷ υἱῷ, **23.** ἵνα πάντες <u>τιμῶσι</u> τὸν υἱὸν καθὼς τιμῶσι τὸν πατέρα. ὁ μὴ τιμῶν τὸν υἱὸν οὐ <u>τιμᾷ</u> τὸν πατέρα τὸν πέμψαντα αὐτόν.

24. Ἀμὴν ἀμὴν λέγω ὑμῖν ὅτι ὁ τὸν λόγον μου ἀκούων καὶ πιστεύων τῷ πέμψαντί με ἔχει ζωὴν αἰώνιον, καὶ εἰς κρίσιν οὐκ ἔρχεται ἀλλὰ μεταβέβηκεν[23] ἐκ τοῦ θανάτου εἰς τὴν ζωήν. **25.** ἀμὴν ἀμὴν λέγω ὑμῖν ὅτι ἔρχεται ὥρα καὶ νῦν ἐστιν ὅτε οἱ νεκροὶ ἀκούσουσιν τῆς φωνῆς τοῦ υἱοῦ τοῦ θεοῦ καὶ οἱ ἀκούσαντες ζήσουσιν. **26.** ὥσπερ γὰρ ὁ πατὴρ ἔχει ζωὴν ἐν ἑαυτῷ, οὕτως καὶ τῷ υἱῷ ἔδωκεν ζωὴν ἔχειν ἐν ἑαυτῷ.

Parsing: δείξει _____

τιμῶσι _____

τιμᾷ _____

Translation: _____

_____

_____

_____

_____

_____

_____

_____

_____

_____

_____

[22]ζῳοποιέω, *I make alive, give life to* (11).   [23]μεταβαίνω, *I go or pass over* (12).

Reading 5 | John 5:27–32

27. καὶ ἐξουσίαν ἔδωκεν αὐτῷ κρίσιν ποιεῖν, ὅτι υἱὸς ἀνθρώπου ἐστίν.

28. μὴ θαυμάζετε τοῦτο, ὅτι ἔρχεται ὥρα ἐν ᾗ πάντες οἱ ἐν τοῖς <u>μνημείοις</u> ἀκούσουσιν τῆς φωνῆς αὐτοῦ **29.** καὶ ἐκπορεύσονται, οἱ τὰ ἀγαθὰ ποιήσαντες εἰς ἀνάστασιν ζωῆς, οἱ δὲ τὰ φαῦλα[24] <u>πράξαντες</u> εἰς ἀνάστασιν κρίσεως. **30.** Οὐ δύναμαι ἐγὼ ποιεῖν ἀπ᾽ ἐμαυτοῦ οὐδέν· καθὼς ἀκούω κρίνω, καὶ ἡ κρίσις ἡ ἐμὴ δικαία ἐστίν, ὅτι οὐ ζητῶ τὸ θέλημα τὸ ἐμὸν ἀλλὰ τὸ θέλημα τοῦ <u>πέμψαντός</u> με.

31. Ἐὰν ἐγὼ μαρτυρῶ περὶ ἐμαυτοῦ, ἡ μαρτυρία μου οὐκ ἔστιν ἀληθής· **32.** ἄλλος ἐστὶν ὁ μαρτυρῶν περὶ ἐμοῦ, καὶ οἶδα ὅτι ἀληθής ἐστιν ἡ μαρτυρία ἣν μαρτυρεῖ περὶ ἐμοῦ.

Parsing: μνημείοις   _____

                  πράξαντες   _____

                  πέμψαντός   _____

Translation: _____

_____

_____

_____

_____

_____

_____

_____

_____

_____

_____

_____

---

[24]φαῦλος, η, ον, _worthless, bad, evil_ (6).

33. ὑμεῖς ἀπεστάλκατε πρὸς Ἰωάννην, καὶ μεμαρτύρηκεν τῇ ἀληθείᾳ· **34.** ἐγὼ δὲ οὐ παρὰ ἀνθρώπου τὴν μαρτυρίαν λαμβάνω, ἀλλὰ ταῦτα λέγω ἵνα ὑμεῖς <u>σωθῆτε</u>. **35.** ἐκεῖνος ἦν ὁ λύχνος[25] ὁ καιόμενος[26] καὶ φαίνων, ὑμεῖς δὲ <u>ἠθελήσατε</u> ἀγαλλιαθῆναι[27] πρὸς ὥραν ἐν τῷ φωτὶ αὐτοῦ.

36. ἐγὼ δὲ ἔχω τὴν μαρτυρίαν μείζω τοῦ Ἰωάννου· τὰ γὰρ ἔργα ἃ δέδωκέν μοι ὁ πατὴρ ἵνα τελειώσω αὐτά, αὐτὰ τὰ ἔργα ἃ ποιῶ, μαρτυρεῖ περὶ ἐμοῦ ὅτι ὁ πατὴρ με ἀπέσταλκεν· **37.** καὶ ὁ πέμψας με πατὴρ ἐκεῖνος μεμαρτύρηκεν περὶ ἐμοῦ. οὔτε φωνὴν αὐτοῦ πώποτε ἀκηκόατε οὔτε εἶδος[28] αὐτοῦ ἑωράκατε, **38.** καὶ τὸν λόγον αὐτοῦ οὐκ ἔχετε ἐν ὑμῖν <u>μένοντα</u>, ὅτι ὃν ἀπέστειλεν ἐκεῖνος τούτῳ ὑμεῖς οὐ πιστεύετε.

Parsing: σωθῆτε _____

ἠθελήσατε _____

μένοντα _____

Translation:

_____

_____

_____

_____

_____

_____

_____

_____

_____

_____

_____

_____

[25]λύχνος, ου, ὁ, *lamp* (14).   [26]καίω, *I light, burn* (12).   [27]ἀγαλλιάω, *I exult, am glad* (11).   [28]εἶδος, ους, τό, *form, appearance* (5).

Vocabulary

Friends	Memory Aids
ἀργύριον, -ου, τό, *silver, money* (20).	Argent—**silver**.
γένος, -ους, τό, *race, descendants* (20).	γενεά—family, generation.
γονεύς, -έως, ὁ, *parent, parents* (20).	Required to have descendants (γένος).
ἑκατοντάρχης, -ου, ὁ, *centurion, officer* (20).	Leader (ἄρχων) of 100 (ἑκατόν).
χιλίαρχος, -ου, ὁ , *military tribune* (21).	Leader (ἄρχων) of 1,000 (χιλιάς).
ἐπίγνωσις, -εως, ἡ, *knowledge, recognition* (20).	γνῶσις—**knowledge**.
ἡγεμών, -όνος, ὁ, *prince, governor* (20).	Hegemony.
Ἰσαάκ, ὁ, *Isaac* (20).	Just like it sounds.
μνημονεύω, *I remember, recall, recollect* (21).	Mnemonic.
νυνί, *now* (20).	νύν—**now**.
πειρασμός, -οῦ, ὁ, *temptation, test* (21).	πειράζω—I **test**, try.
προάγω, *I lead forward, go or come before* (20).	I **lead** (ἄγω) **before** (πρό).
σοφός, -ή, -όν, *clever, wise* (20).	σοφία—wisdom.
τελώνης, -ου, ὁ, *tax collector* (21).	τελός—**tax**, end, goal.
τιμάω, *I honor, set a price on* (21).	τιμή—**honor**.
ὑπακούω, *I obey, follow* (21).	ἀκούω—I hear, **obey**.
ὡσεί, *as, like, about* (21).	ὡς—**as, like**.
Cousins	
ἰχθύς, -ύος, ὁ, *fish* (20).	Ichthyology—study of **fish**; ichthys, an ancient icon/acronym of Jesus.
Strangers	
αἰτία, -ας, ἡ, *cause, reason, accusation* (20).	Aetiology—the study of the **causes** of disease.
ἀκροβυστία, ας, ἡ, *foreskin, uncircumcision* (20).	
νηστεύω, *I fast* (20).	I no—ἐσθίω (eat).
ξύλον, -ου, τό, *wood, tree* (20).	Xylophone—a sound made from a **wood** instrument.
σκηνή, -ῆς, ἡ, *tent, tabernacle* (20).	We will need a skein of thread to mend the **tent**.
τοσοῦτος, -αύτη, -οῦτον, *so great, so much* (20).	
τρέχω, *I run, rush* (20).	A fast trek is a **run**.
ὑπηρέτης, -ου, ὁ, *servant, assistant* (20).	
ὑψόω, *I lift up, exalt* (20).	Hypsometer (a device for measuring height)

Translations

Reading 1   1 John 3:22–24

αἰτῶμεν	1st pl pres act subj, αἰτέω
αὕτη	nom sg fem, οὗτος
τηρῶν	nom sg masc pres act part, τηρέω

22. And whatever we ask, we receive from him, because we keep his commandments and we do the things pleasing in his sight. 23. And this is his commandment, that we believe on the name of his Son, Jesus Christ, and love one another, as he gave a commandment to us. 24. And the one who keeps his commandments, remains in him and he in him; and by this we will know that he remains in us, from the Spirit which[1] he gave to us.

Reading 2   1 John 4:1–6

ἐξεληλύθασιν	3d pl perf act ind, ἐξέρχομαι
ἐληλυθότα	acc sg masc perf act part, ἔρχομαι
ἀκηκόατε	2d pl perf act ind, ἀκούω

1. Beloved, do not believe every spirit, but test the spirits [to see] if they are from God, because many false prophets have gone out into the world. 2. By this you know the spirit of God; every spirit which confesses Jesus Christ having come in the flesh is from God. 3. And every spirit which does not confess Jesus is not from God; and this one is the [spirit] of the antichrist, whom you have heard that it is coming, and now is in the world already.

4. You are from God, children, and you have conquered them, because greater is the one in you than the one in the world. 5. They are from the world; on account of this, they speak from the world and the world hears them.[2] 6. We are from God; the one who knows God hears us, [the one] who is not from God does not hear us. From this we know the spirit of truth and the spirit of deception.

Reading 3   1 John 4:7–11

ἀγαπητοί	voc[3] pl masc, ἀγαπητός
ἠγαπήκαμεν	1st pl perf act ind, ἀγαπάω
ἀγαπᾶν	pres act inf, ἀγαπάω

7. Beloved, let us love one another, because love is from God, and everyone who loves has been born from God and knows God. 8. The one who does not love does not know God, because God is love. 9. By this the love of God was revealed among us, that God has sent his one and only Son into the world so that we might live through him. 10. Love is [demonstrated] in this, not that we have loved God, but that he loved us and sent his Son [as] an atoning sacrifice, for our sins. 11. Beloved, if in this way God loved us, also we ought to love one another.

Reading 4   1 John 4:12–16a

δέδωκεν	3d sg perf act ind, δίδωμι
μαρτυροῦμεν	1st pl pres act ind, μαρτυρέω
ἥν	acc sg fem, ὅς

12. No one has ever seen God; if we love each other, God remains in us and his love is made perfect in us.

13. By this we know that we remain in him and he in us, that he has given to us from his Spirit. 14. And we have seen and we bear witness that the Father has sent the Son [as] Savior of the world. 15. Whoever confesses that Jesus is the Son of God, God remains in him, and he in God. 16. And we have known and we have believed the love which God has in us.

Reading 5   1 John 4:16b–21

κρίσεως	gen sg fem, κρίσις
ἔξω	adverb, ἔξω
ἀγαπᾷ	3d sg pres act subj, ἀγαπάω

16b. God is love, and the one who remains in love remains in God, and God remains in him. 17. By this, love has been perfected with us, so that we might have boldness in the day of judgment, because as that one is, also we are in this world. 18. Fear is not in love, but perfect love casts out fear, because fear has punishment, and the one who fears has not been perfected in love.

19. We love because he first loved us. 20. If anyone says, "I love God," and hates his brother, he is a liar; for the one

---

[1] οὗ is in the genitive case because of attraction (*BBG*, 114).   [2] αὐτῶν is in the genitive case because ἀκούω may take its object in the genitive case (*BBG*, 131).   [3] The case used for direct address (*BBG*, 105).

who does not love his brother whom he has seen is not able to love God whom he has not seen. 21. And this commandment we have from him, that the one who loves God loves also his brother.

Reading 6   1 John 5:1–6

γεγεννημένον	acc sg masc perf mid/pass part, γεννάω
ὕδατι	dat sg neut, ὕδωρ
μαρτυροῦν	nom sg neut pres act part, μαρτυρέω

1. Everyone who believes that Jesus is the Christ has been begotten from God, and everyone who loves the one who

begets, loves also the one who has been begotten from him. 2. By this we know that we love the children of God, when we love God and do his commandments. 3. For this is the love of God, that we might keep his commandments; and his commandments are not oppressive, 4. because everything which has been born from God conquers the world; and this is the victory which conquers the world, [namely] our faith. 5. And who is the one who conquers the world except the one who believes that Jesus is the Son of God?

6. This is the one who comes through water and blood, Jesus Christ; not by water only, but by the water and by the blood; and the Spirit is the one who bears witness, because the Spirit is the truth.

Week Two

Reading 1   John 16:1–6

ποιήσουσιν	3ᵈ pl fut act ind, ποιέω
δόξῃ	3ᵈ sg aor act subj, δοκέω
ἤμην	1ˢᵗ sg impf act ind, εἰμί
ἐρωτᾷ	3ᵈ sg pres act ind, ἐρωτάω

1. "I have said these things to you so that you may not stumble. 2. They will make you [ones] expelled from the synagogue; but an hour is coming that everyone who kills you will think that he is offering service to God.[4] 3. And they will do these things because they did not know the Father nor me. 4. But these things I have spoken to you so that whenever the hour comes, you might remember that I said [them] to you.

But these things I did not say to you from the beginning because I was with you. 5. But now I depart to the one who has sent me, and not one of you asks me, 'Where are you going?' 6. But because I have spoken these things to you, grief has filled your heart."

Reading 2   John 16:7–11

ἐλεύσεται	3ᵈ sg fut mid ind, ἔρχομαι
ἐλθὼν	nom sg masc aor act part, ἔρχομαι
ἐμέ	acc sg, ἐγώ

7. "But I speak the truth to you, it is good for you that I depart. For if I do not depart, the intercessor will not come to you; but if I go, I will send him to you. 8. And that one when he comes will convict the world concerning sin and concerning righteousness and concerning judg-

ment; 9. concerning sin, on the one hand, because they do not believe in me; 10. concerning righteousness, on the other hand, because I am going to the Father and no longer [will] you see me; 11. and concerning judgment, because the ruler of this world has been judged."

Reading 3   John 16:12–16

ἀκούσει	3ᵈ sg fut act ind, ἀκούω
λήμψεται	3ᵈ sg fut mid ind, λαμβάνω
ὄψεσθε	2ᵈ pl fut mid ind, ὁράω

12. "Still I have many things to say to you, but you are not able to comprehend [them] now; 13. but when that one comes, the Spirit of truth, he will lead you in all truth; for he will not speak from himself, but whatever he will hear, he will speak, and he will announce the coming things to you. 14. That one will glorify me, because he will receive from [the thing] of me and will announce [it] to you. 15. All things which the Father has are mine; because of this I said that he receives from [the thing] of me and he will report [it] to you.

16. A little while and you see me no longer, and again a little while and you will see me."

Reading 4   John 16:17–22

ἔγνω	3ᵈ sg aor act ind, γινώσκω
ἤθελον	3ᵈ pl impf act ind, θέλω
χαρήσεται	3ᵈ sg fut pass ind, χαίρω

17. Therefore, [some] of his disciples said to one another, "What is this that he says to us, 'A little while and you do not see me, and again a little while and you will see

---

[4]See Wallace, 604.

me' and 'because I am going to the Father'?" 18. Then they were saying, "What is this that he says, the 'a little while'? We do not understand what he says."

19. Jesus knew that they were wishing to ask him, and he said to them, "Do you seek with one another concerning this thing because I said 'A little while and you do not see me, and again a little while and you will see me?' 20. Truly, truly, I say to you that you will weep and you will lament, but the world will rejoice. You will be grieved, but your grief will become joy. 21. When a woman is in labor she has pain, because her hour came; but when she gives birth to a child, she no longer remembers the anguish on account of the joy because a person was born into the world. 22. And therefore you now indeed have grief; but I will see you again, and your heart will rejoice, and no one takes your joy from you."

Reading 5 — John 16:23–27

ἐρωτήσετε	2ᵈ pl fut act ind, ἐρωτάω
δώσει	3ᵈ sg, fut act ind, δίδωμι
ἦ	3ᵈ sg pres act subj, εἰμί

23. "And you will not ask me anything on that day. Truly, truly, I say to you, whatever you ask the Father in my name, he will give to you. 24. Until now you asked nothing in my name; ask and you will receive that your joy may be full.

25. I have spoken these things in parables to you; the hour comes when no longer in parables will I speak to you, but with boldness concerning the Father will I report to you. 26. In that day you will ask in my name, and I do not say to you that I will ask the Father concerning you; 27. for the Father himself loves you, because you have loved me and you have believed that I came forth from God.

Reading 6 — John 16:28–33

ἐρωτᾷ	3ᵈ sg pres act subj, ἐρωτάω
ἐλήλυθεν	3ᵈ sg perf act ind, ἔρχομαι
ἀφῆτε	2ᵈ pl aor act subj, ἀφίημι

28. "I came forth from the Father and I have come into the world; again I am leaving the world and going to the Father." 29. His disciples said, "Behold, now you speak with boldness, and you speak not one parable. 30. Now we know that you know all things and you do not have need that anyone question you. We believe by this that you came forth from God."

31. Jesus answered them, "Now you believe? 32. Behold, an hour comes and it has come that you might be scattered, each to his own things, and you might leave me alone; and I am not alone, because the Father is with me.

33. These things I have spoken to you that you might have peace in me; in the world you have tribulation, but be of good cheer, I have conquered the world."

Week Three

Reading 1 — Matthew 16:13–17

μέρη	acc pl neut, μέρος
ἠρώτα	3ᵈ sg impf act ind, ἐρωτάω
ἕνα	acc sg masc, εἷς

13. And Jesus, coming into the parts of Caesarea of Philip, was questioning his disciples, saying, "Who do the people say the Son of Man is?"

14. And they said, "Some [say] John the Baptist, and others [say] Elijah, and others [say] Jeremiah, or one of the prophets."

15. He said to them, "But you, who do you say I am?"[5]

16. And answering, Simon Peter said, "You are the Christ, the Son of the living God."

17. And answering, Jesus said to him, "Blessed are you, Simon Bar-Jona, because flesh and blood did not reveal to you, but my Father, the one in heaven."[6]

Reading 2 — Matthew 16:18–22

δώσω	1ˢᵗ sg fut act ind, δίδωμι
δήσῃς	2ᵈ sg aor act subj, δέω
ἤρξατο	3ᵈ sg aor mid ind, ἄρχω

18. "And also I say to you that you are Peter, and upon this rock I will build my church and the gates of Hades shall not prevail against it. 19. I will give to you the keys of the kingdom of heaven, and whatever you bind on the earth will be bound in heaven, and whatever you loose on earth

---

[5]You will notice that we have translated the infinitive εἶναι (vv. 13, 15) in two different ways. This was done to make a smooth translation. Literally the verses would read, *who do people say the Son of Man to be?* (v. 13) and *who do you say me to be?* (v. 15).   [6]In classical Greek, οὐρανός was always a singular noun, *heaven*. The use of the plural forms reflects a Semitic intensive plural or plural of extension, in which certain objects are viewed in their intensity. We have elected to translate both singular and plural forms of οὐρανός as *heaven*, omitting the article when necessary.

will be loosed in heaven." 20. Then he warned the disciples that to no one they should say that he is the Christ.

21. From then on Jesus began to explain to his disciples that it was necessary for him to depart to Jerusalem and to suffer many things from the elders and high priests and scribes, and to be killed, and on the third day to be raised.

22. And, taking him aside, Peter began to rebuke him saying, "God forbid, Lord; this thing will never be to you."

Reading 3   Matthew 16:23–28

εἶ	2ᵈ sg pres act ind, εἰμί
σῶσαι	aor act inf, σῴζω
ἴδωσιν	3ᵈ pl aor act subj, ὁράω

23. And turning, he said to Peter, "Go behind me, Satan; you are a trap to me, because you do not think the things of God but the things of humans."

24. Then Jesus said to his disciples, "If anyone wants to come after me, let him deny himself and take up his cross and follow me. 25. For whoever wants to save his life will lose it; but whoever loses his life because of me, will find it. 26. For in what way will a person be helped if he gains the whole world but forfeits his life? Or what will a person give in exchange for his life? 27. For the Son of Man is about to come in the glory of his Father with his angels, and then he will give out [a reward] to each according to his conduct. 28. Truly, I say to you that there are certain ones of those standing here who will not taste death until they see the Son of Man coming into his kingdom."

Reading 4   Matthew 17:1–5

ὤφθη	3ᵈ sg aor pass ind, ὁράω
μίαν	acc sg fem, εἷς
ᾧ	dat sg masc, ὅς

1. And after six days, Jesus took Peter and James and John, his brother, and led them up to a high mountain, privately.

2. And he was changed before them, and his face shone as the sun, and his garments became white as the light. 3. And behold, Moses and Elijah appeared to them, conversing with him.

4. And answering, Peter said to Jesus, "Lord, it is good for us to be here; if you wish, I will make three shelters here, one for you, one for Moses, and one for Elijah."

5. While he was still speaking, behold, a bright cloud overshadowed them and behold, [there was] a voice from the cloud saying, "This is my beloved son, in whom I am well pleased; listen to him."

Reading 5   Matthew 17:6–10

ἔπεσαν	3ᵈ pl aor act ind, πίπτω
ἐφοβήθησαν	3ᵈ pl aor pass ind, φοβέω
μηδενί	dat sg masc, μηδείς

6. And hearing, the disciples fell upon their faces and were greatly afraid. 7. And Jesus went forward and touching them said, "Rise and do not be afraid." 8. And raising their eyes, they saw no one except Jesus himself, only.

9. And while they were descending from the mountain, Jesus commanded them, saying, "To no one tell the vision until the Son of Man has been raised from the dead."

10. And the disciples questioned him, saying, "Why then do the scribes say that it is necessary for Elijah to come first?"

Reading 6   Matthew 17:11–16

ἠθέλησαν	3ᵈ pl aor act ind, θέλω
προσήνεγκα	1ˢᵗ sg aor act ind, προσφέρω
θεραπεῦσαι	aor act inf, θεραπεύω

11. And he, answering, said, "Elijah indeed comes and he will restore all things; 12. but I say to you that Elijah already came and they did not recognize him, but they did to him what things they wished; in this manner also the Son of Man is about to suffer by them." 13. Then the disciples understood that he spoke to them concerning John the Baptist.

14. And when they came to the crowd, a man came to him, falling on his knees [before] him 15. and saying, "Lord, have mercy on my son, because he is a lunatic and suffers severely; for many times he falls into the fire and many times into the water. 16. And I brought him to your disciples, and they were not able to heal him."

Week Four

Reading 1   John 6:25–29

γέγονας	2ᵈ sg perf act ind, γίνομαι
ἐφάγετε	2ᵈ pl aor act ind, ἐσθίω
μένουσαν	acc sg fem pres act part, μένω

25. And finding him on the other side of the sea, they said to him, "Rabbi, when did you come here?"

26. Jesus answered them and said, "Truly, truly, I say to you, you seek me not because you saw signs, but because

you ate from the loaves and were filled. 27. Work not for the food that perishes, but the food that endures to eternal life, which the Son of Man will give to you; for the Father, God, put a seal on this one."

28. Thus they said to him, "What must we do that we might work the works of God?"

29. Jesus answered and said to them, "This is the work of God, that you believe in the one whom that one sent."

Reading 2   John 6:30–35

σοι	dat sg pronoun, σύ
δέδωκεν	3d sg perf act ind, δίδωμι
διδούς	nom sg masc pres act part, δίδωμι

30. Therefore they said to him, "Then what sign do you do that we might see and believe in you? What work do you do? 31. Our fathers ate manna in the wilderness, as it has been written, 'He gave bread from heaven to them to eat.'"

32. So Jesus said to them, "Truly, truly, I say to you, Moses has not given the bread from heaven to you, but my Father gives to you the true bread from heaven; 33. for the bread of God is he who descends from heaven and gives life to the world."

34. Therefore they said to him, "Lord, always give this bread to us."

35. Jesus said to them, "I am the bread of life. The one who comes to me will not hunger, and the one who believes in me will never thirst at all."[7]

Reading 3   John 6:36–40

ἐκβάλω	1st sg aor act subj, ἐκβάλλω
ἀναστήσω	1st sg fut act ind, ἀνίστημι
ἔχῃ	3d sg pres act subj, ἔχω

36. "But I said to you that both you have seen me and you do not believe. 37. Everything the Father gives to me will come to me, and the one coming to me, I will not cast outside, 38. because I have descended from heaven not that I might do my will, but the will of the one who sent me; 39. and this is the will of the one who sent me, that everything he has given to me I will not lose [any] of it, but I will raise it in the last day. 40. For this is the will of my Father, that everyone who sees the Son and believes in him has eternal life, and I will raise him up in the last day."

Reading 4   John 6:41–46

καταβάς	nom sg masc aor act part, καταβαίνω
ἐλθεῖν	aor act inf, ἔρχομαι
γεγραμμένον	nom sg neut perf mid/pass part, γράφω

41. Thus the Jews were grumbling concerning him because he said, "I am the bread that descended from heaven." 42. And they were saying, "Is this not Jesus, the son of Joseph, whose father and mother we know? How now does he say, 'From heaven I have descended'?"

43. Jesus answered and said to them, "Do not grumble with one another. 44. No one is able to come to me unless the Father who sent me should draw him, and I will raise him in the last day. 45. It has been written in the prophets, 'And all will be instructed [by] God.' Everyone who hears from the Father and learns comes to me. 46. [It is] not that anyone has seen the Father, except the one being from God, this one has seen the Father."

Reading 5   John 6:47–53

ἀπέθανον	3d pl aor act ind, ἀποθνῄσκω
φάγῃ	3d sg aor act subj, ἐσθίω
δοῦναι	aor act inf, δίδωμι

47. "Truly, truly, I say to you, the one who believes has eternal life. 48. I am the bread of life. 49. Your fathers ate manna in the desert and they died; 50. This is the bread that descends from heaven so that anyone might eat of it and not die. 51. I am the living bread that descended from heaven; if anyone eats from this bread, he will live forever;[8] and also the bread that I will give, on behalf of the life of the world, is my flesh."

52. Thus the Jews were quarreling with one another, saying, "How is this man able to give to us his flesh to eat?"

53. Therefore Jesus said to them, "Truly, truly, I say to you, unless you eat the flesh of the Son of Man and drink his blood, you do not have life in yourselves."

Reading 6   John 6:54–59

πίνων	nom sg masc pres act part, πίνω
ζῶ	1st sg pres act ind, ζάω
οὐρανοῦ	gen sg masc, οὐρανός

---

[7]Wallace notes that οὐ μή plus an aorist subjunctive is used to express emphatic negation (the strongest negation in Greek). Less frequently, however, οὐ μή is found with a verb in the future indicative to express this emphatic negation (Wallace, 468). [8]εἰς τὸν αἰῶνα, literally translated as "into the age," is an idiom that is often rendered *forever* (BAGD, s.v. αἰών, 1.b).

54. "The one who eats my flesh and drinks my blood has eternal life, and I will raise him in the last day; 55. for my flesh is true food and my blood is true drink. 56. The one who eats my flesh and drinks my blood remains in me and I in him. 57. As the living Father sent me and I live because of the Father, also the one who eats me, even that one, will live because of me. 58. This is the bread that descended from heaven, not as the fathers ate and died; the one who eats this bread will live forever." 59. He said these things while teaching in the synagogue in Capernaum.

Week Five

Reading 1	John 12:44–50
ἐλήλυθα	1st sg perf act ind, ἔρχομαι
μείνῃ	3d sg aor act subj, μένω
κρίνοντα	acc sg masc pres act part, κρίνω

44. But Jesus cried out and said, "The one who believes in me does not believe in me but in the one who sent me, 45. and the one who sees me sees the one who sent me. 46. I, [as] a light, have come into the world, so that everyone who believes in me might not remain in the darkness.

47. And if anyone hears my words and does not keep [them], I do not judge him; for I did not come that I might judge the world, but that I might save the world. 48. The one who sets me aside and who does not receive my words has the one judging him; the word which I spoke, that will judge him in the last day. 49. Because I did not speak from myself, but the one who sent me, the Father himself, has given a commandment to me, what I should say and what I should speak. 50. And I know that his commandment is eternal life. Therefore [the things] that I speak, as the Father has spoken to me, thus I speak."

Reading 2	John 13:1–6
εἰδώς	nom sg masc perf act part, οἶδα
βεβληκότος	gen sg masc perf act part, βάλλω
παραδοῖ	3d sg aor act subj, παραδίδωμι

1. And before the feast of the Passover, Jesus, knowing that his hour had come so that he might go from this world to the Father, having loved [his] own who [were] in the world, to [the] end he loved them.

2. And dinner being [served], the devil already having put into the heart of Judas [son] of Simon Iscariot that he should betray him, 3. knowing that the Father gave all things to him into [his] hands and that from God he came forth and to God he goes, 4. he rose from the dinner and put [aside] [his] garments, and taking a towel tied it around himself. 5. Then he put water into the washbasin and began to wash the feet of the disciples and to wipe [them] dry with the towel with which he was tied around.

6. Then he came to Simon Peter. He said to him, "Lord, do you wash my feet?"

Reading 3	John 13:7–11
γνώσῃ	2d sg fut mid ind, γινώσκω
ἐμοῦ	gen sg pronoun, ἐγώ
παραδιδόντα	acc sg masc pres act part, παραδίδωμι

7. Jesus answered and said to him, "That which I do, you do not understand now, but you will know after these things."

8. Peter said to him, "You will not wash my feet forever." Jesus answered to him, "Unless I wash you, you do not have a portion with me."

9. Simon Peter said to him, "Lord, not my feet alone, but also [my] hands and [my] head."

10. Jesus said to him, "The one having been bathed does not have need to wash [anything] except the feet, but he is completely clean; and you [disciples] are clean, but not all [of you]." 11. For he knew the one betraying him; on account of this he said "Not all [of you] are clean."

Reading 4	John 13:12–18
πεποίηκα	1st sg perf act ind, ποιέω
ἔδωκα	1st sg aor act ind, δίδωμι
μακάριοι	nom pl masc, μακάριος

12. Then, when he washed their feet, he took his garments and reclined again, he said to them, "Do you know what I have done to you? 13. You call me 'the Teacher' and 'the Lord,' and you speak well, for I am. 14. Therefore if I, the Lord and the Teacher, washed your feet, also you ought to wash the feet of one another. 15. For I gave an example to you in order that as I did to you also you might do. 16. Truly, truly, I say to you, a servant is not greater than his master nor an apostle greater than the one who sent him. 17. If you know these things, you are blessed if you do them.

18. I do not speak concerning all of you; I know whom I chose; but in order that the scripture might be fulfilled, 'The one who eats my bread lifted up his heel against me.'"

Reading 5	John 13:19–25
πέμψω	1st sg aor act subj, πέμπω
ἐμαρτύρησεν	3d sg aor act ind, μαρτυρέω
ἠγάπα	3d sg impf act ind, ἀγαπάω

19. "From now I speak to you before [it] happens, so that you might believe when it happens that I am. 20. Truly, truly, I say to you, the one who receives whomever I may send receives me, and the one who receives me receives the one who sent me."

21. After saying these things, Jesus was disturbed in the spirit and he testified and said, "Truly, truly, I say to you that one of you will betray me."

22. The disciples were looking at each other, being at a loss concerning whom he was speaking. 23. One from his disciples was reclining on the chest of Jesus, whom Jesus loved; 24. then Simon Peter motioned to this one to ask who it might be concerning whom he was speaking.

25. Therefore that one, reclining thus on the chest of Jesus, said to him, "Lord, who is it?"

Reading 6   **John 13:26–30**

ποίησον	2d sg aor act impt, ποιέω
ἔγνω	3d sg aor act ind, γινώσκω
εἶχεν	3d sg impf act ind, ἔχω

26. Jesus answered, "It is that one for whom I will dip the piece of bread and give it to him." So, dipping the piece of bread, he gave [it] to Judas, [son] of Simon Iscariot. 27. And after the piece of bread, then Satan entered into that one. Then Jesus said to him, "That which you do, do quickly." 28. But none of the ones reclining knew this for what [reason] he spoke to him; 29. for some were thinking, because Judas kept the money box, that Jesus said to him, "Purchase [the things] of which we have need for the feast" or that he should give something to the poor. 30. Therefore after taking the piece of bread, that one immediately went out; and it was night.

Week Six

Reading 1   **John 13:31–35**

ἐδοξάσθη	3d sg aor pass ind, δοξάζω
δοξάσει	3d sg fut act ind, δοξάζω
Ἰουδαίοις	dat pl masc, Ἰουδαῖος

31. Therefore when he went out, Jesus said, "Now the Son of Man is glorified, and God is glorified in him; 32. if God is glorified in him God will also glorify him in him and immediately will glorify him.

33. Children, I am with you yet a little [longer]; you will seek me, and as I said to the Jews, 'Where I go, you are not able to go,' also I say to you now.

34. I give a new commandment to you, that you love one another; as I loved you that also you love one another. 35. By this all will know that you are disciples to me, if you have love among one another."

Reading 2   **John 13:36–14:4**

ἀκολουθήσεις	2d sg fut act ind, ἀκολουθέω
θήσω	1st sg fut act ind, τίθημι
φωνήσῃ	3d sg aor act subj, φωνέω

36. Simon Peter said to him, "Lord, where are you going?" Jesus answered, "Where I go you are not able to follow me now, but you will follow later."

37. Peter said to him, "Lord, why am I not able to follow you now? I will lay down my life for you."

38. Jesus answered, "Will you lay down your life for me? Truly, truly, I say to you, the rooster will not call out until you deny me three times."

14:1 "Let your heart not be troubled; believe[9] in God; also believe in me. 2. In my Father's house are many rooms; and if not, would I have said to you that I go to prepare a place for you? 3. And if I go and prepare a place for you, I am coming again and I will take you to myself, so that where I am also you may be. 4. And where I go, you know the way."

Reading 3   **John 14:5–10**

εἰδέναι	perf act inf, οἶδα
δεῖξον	2d sg aor act impt, δείκνυμι
ἑωρακὼς	nom sg masc perf act part, ὁράω

5. Thomas said to him, "Lord, we do not know where you go; how are we able to know the way?"

6. Jesus said to him, "I am the way and the truth and the life; no one comes to the Father except through me. 7. If you have known me, also you will know my Father; and from now you know him and have seen him."

8. Philip said to him, "Lord, show the Father to us, and it is sufficient for us."

9. Jesus said to him, "Am I with you for so long a time and you have not known me, Philip? The one who has seen me has seen the Father; how do you say, 'Show the Father

---

[9]This verb could also be an indicative.

to us?' 10. Do you not believe that I [am] in the Father and the Father is in me? The words that I say to you, I do not speak from myself; but the Father who remains in me does his works.

Reading 4   John 14:11–17

ἅ	acc pl neut, ὅς
αἰτήσητέ	2ᵈ pl aor act subj, αἰτέω
θεωρεῖ	3ᵈ sg pres act ind, θεωρέω

11. "Believe me that I [am] in the Father and the Father [is] in me; and if not, believe on account of the works themselves. 12. Truly, truly, I say to you, the one who believes in me, the works which I do, that one also will do, and he will do greater [works] than these, because I go to the Father; 13. and whatever you ask in my name, this I will do, so that the Father might be glorified in the Son; 14. if you ask me anything in my name I will do [it].

15. If you love me, you will keep my commandments; 16. and I will ask the Father and he will give another intercessor to you, so that he may be with you forever, 17. [namely] the Spirit of truth, whom the world is not able to receive, because it does not see him[10] nor does it know [him]. You know him since he dwells with you and he will be in you."

Reading 5   John 14:18–24

ζῶ	1ˢᵗ sg pres act ind, ζάω
ἀγαπηθήσεται	3ᵈ sg fut pass ind, ἀγαπάω
ἐλευσόμεθα	1ˢᵗ pl fut mid ind, ἔρχομαι

18. "I will not leave you orphans, I am coming to you. 19. Yet a little [longer] and the world no longer sees me, but you see me; because I live also you will live. 20. In that day you will know that I [am] in my Father and you [are]

in me, and I [am] in you. 21. The one who has my commandments and who keeps them, that one is the one who loves me; and the one who loves me will be loved by my Father and I will love him and I will reveal myself to him."

22. Judas (not the Iscariot) said to him, "Lord, and what has happened that you intend to reveal yourself to us and not to the world?"

23. Jesus answered and said to him, "If anyone loves me he will keep my word, and my Father will love him, and we will come to him and we will make [an] abode with him. 24. The one who does not love me does not keep my words; and the word that you hear is not mine but [the word] of the Father who sent me."

Reading 6   John 14:25–31

εἰρήνην	acc sg fem, εἰρήνη
ἐχάρητε	2ᵈ pl aor pass ind, χαίρω
γένηται	3ᵈ sg aor mid subj, γίνομαι

25. "These things I have spoken to you [while] remaining with you. 26. But the intercessor, the Holy Spirit, whom the Father will send in my name, that one will teach you all things and will remind you [of] all that I said to you. 27. I leave peace with you; my peace I give to you; not as the world gives do I give to you. Let not your heart be troubled nor let it be timid.

28. You heard that I said to you, 'I depart and come to you'; if you had loved me, you would have rejoiced because I go to the Father, because the Father is greater than I. 29. And now I have told you before it happens, so that when it happens, you may believe. 30. No longer will I speak many things with you, for the ruler of the world comes; and in me he does not have anything, 31. but in order that the world might know that I love the Father and as the Father commanded me, so I do. Arise, let us go from here."

Week Seven

Reading 1   Matthew 26:27–31

πίετε	2ᵈ pl aor act impt, πίνω
διαθήκης	gen sg fem, διαθήκη
σκανδαλισθήσεσθε	2ᵈ pl fut pass ind, σκανδαλίζω

27. And after taking a cup and giving thanks, he gave [it] to them saying, "All [of you] drink from this, 28. for

this is my blood of the covenant which is poured out for many for [the] pardon of sins. 29. But I say to you, I definitely won't drink from now [on] of this fruit of the vine until that day when I drink it with you anew in the kingdom of my Father."

30. And after singing a hymn, they went out to the Mount of Olives.

---

[10]The pronoun αὐτό is neuter, but the Spirit, at least in evangelical circles, has always been seen as a person; thus is it appropriate to translate this pronoun as "him." The reason for the neuter is, of course, because πνεῦμα is neuter. Note also the masculine ἐκεῖνος in verse 26, which refers to τὸ πνεῦμα τὸ ἅγιον.

31. Then Jesus said to them, "All of you will fall[11] away because of me in this night, for it has been written, 'I will strike the shepherd and the sheep of the flock will be scattered.'"

Reading 2   Matthew 26:32–37

ἔφη	3ᵈ sg imperf *or* aor act ind, φημί
φωνῆσαι	aor act inf, φωνέω
δέη	3ᵈ sg pres act subj, δεῖ

32. "But after I am raised, I will go before you into Galilee."

33. And answering, Peter said to him, "[Even] if all are repelled by you, I will never be repelled."

34. Jesus said to him, "Truly, I say to you that in this night before a rooster calls out you will deny me three times."

35. Peter said to him, "Even if it is necessary for me to die with you, I will definitely not deny you." Likewise also all the disciples said.

36. Then Jesus came with them to a place called Gethsemane, and he said to the disciples, "Sit here while, after going there, I pray." 37. And taking Peter and the two sons of Zebedee he began to be grieved and be troubled.

Reading 3   Matthew 26:38–43

ἔπεσεν	3ᵈ sg aor act ind, πίπτω
προσεύχεσθε	2ᵈ pl pres mid/pass impt, προσεύχομαι
παρελθεῖν	aor act inf, παρέρχομαι

38. Then he said to them, "My soul is deeply grieved unto death; stay here and be watchful with me."

39. And after proceeding a little [way] he fell on his face praying and saying, "My Father, if it is possible, let pass from me this cup; yet not as I will but as you [will]."

40. And he came to the disciples and found them sleeping, and he said to Peter, "So you were not able to be awake one hour with me? 41. Watch and pray, so that you may not enter into temptation; the spirit, on the one hand, is willing, but the flesh, on the other hand, is weak."

42. Again after departing a second [time] he prayed saying, "My Father, if this [cup] cannot pass away except I drink it, [then] let your will come about."

43. And after coming again, he found them sleeping, for their eyes were weighed down.

Reading 4   Matthew 26:44–49

ἤγγικεν	3ᵈ sg perf act ind, ἐγγίζω
παραδίδοται	3ᵈ sg pres mid/pass ind, παραδίδωμι
χαῖρε	2ᵈ sg pres act impt, χαίρω

44. And after leaving them again, going away, he prayed a third time saying the same word again.

45. Then he came to the disciples and said to them, "Are you still sleeping and resting? Behold, the hour has come near and the Son of Man is given over into the hands of sinners. 46. Rise, let us be going; behold, the one betraying me has come near."

47. And while he was still speaking, behold, Judas, one of the twelve came and with him a large crowd, with swords and clubs, from the chief priests and elders of the people. 48. And the one betraying him gave to them a sign, saying, "Whomever I kiss, he is [the one]; seize him." 49. And immediately coming forward, he said to Jesus, "Greetings, Rabbi," and he kissed him.

Reading 5   Matthew 26:50–56

ἀπολοῦνται	3ᵈ pl fut mid ind, ἀπόλλυμι
παραστήσει	3ᵈ sg fut act ind, παρίστημι
πληρωθῶσιν	3ᵈ pl aor pass subj, πληρόω

50. But Jesus said to him, "Friend, [do that] for which you are present." Then after approaching, they laid [their] hands on Jesus and seized him. 51. And behold, one of the ones with Jesus stretching out [his] hand pulled out his sword, and, striking the servant of the high priest, he cut off his ear.

52. Then Jesus said to him, "Return your sword into its place, for all those taking the sword will perish by [the] sword. 53. Or do you think that I am not able to call my Father, and he will place beside me right now more than twelve legions of angels? 54. Then how might be fulfilled the scriptures [that say] that it is necessary to happen in this way?"

55. In that hour Jesus said to the crowds, "As against a robber have you come out with swords and clubs to arrest me? Daily I sat teaching in the temple and you did not arrest me. 56. But this all has come to be so that the writings of the prophets might be fulfilled." Then all the disciples, deserting him, fled.

Reading 6   Matthew 26:57–63

κρατήσαντες	nom pl masc aor act part, κρατέω
συνήχθησαν	3ᵈ pl aor pass ind, συνάγω
τριῶν	gen pl fem, τρεῖς

57. But the ones who arrested Jesus led [him] away to Caiaphas, the high priest, where the scribes and elders were gathered. 58. But Peter was following him from a distance

[11]See BAGD, s.v. σκανδαλίζω, 1.b.

as far as the courtyard of the high priest, and after going inside, he was sitting with the servants to see the outcome.

59. And the high priests and the entire Sanhedrin were seeking false testimony against Jesus in order that they might kill him, 60. and they did not find [any] though many false witnesses were coming forward. But later, two, after coming forward, 61. said, "This [man] said, 'I am able

to tear down the temple of God and after three days to rebuild [it].'"

62. And rising up the high priest said to him, "Do you answer nothing [with regard to] what these [men] are testifying against you?" 63. But Jesus was [keeping] silent. And the high priest said to him, "I adjure you, by the living God, that you tell us if you are the Christ, the Son of God."

Week Eight

Reading 1   Matthew 22:20–25

ἀπόδοτε	2ᵈ pl aor act impt, ἀποδίδωμι
ἀποθάνῃ	3ᵈ sg aor act subj, ἀποθνῄσκω
γήμας	nom sg masc aor act part, γαμέω

20. And he said to them, "Of whom [is] this image and [this] inscription?"

21. They said to him, "Of Caesar." Then he said to them, "Then pay back the things of Caesar to Caesar and the things of God to God."

22. And hearing, they marveled, and leaving him they went away.

23. On that day Sadducees, who say there is not a resurrection, came to him, and they questioned him 24. saying, "Teacher, Moses said, 'If a certain man dies not having children, his brother will marry as next of kin his wife and raise up offspring for his brother.' 25. And there were with us seven brothers; and the first, after marrying, died, and not having offspring, he left his wife to his brother;

Reading 2   Matthew 22:26–33

ἀπέθανεν	3ᵈ sg aor act ind, ἀποθνῄσκω
πλανᾶσθε	2ᵈ pl pres mid/pass ind, πλανάω
ῥηθὲν	acc sg neut aor pass part, λέγω

26. "Likewise also the second and the third, until the [last] of the seven. 27. And last of all, the woman died. 28. Therefore, in the resurrection, of which of the seven will she be [the] wife? For all had her."

29. And Jesus answering said to them, "You are deceived, not knowing the Scriptures nor the power of God; 30. for in the resurrection, they neither marry nor are given in marriage, but they are as angels in heaven. 31. But concerning the resurrection of the dead did you not read the [thing] that was said to you by God, saying, 32. 'I am the God of Abraham and the God of Isaac and the God of Jacob'? He is not the God of the dead but of the living."

33. And after hearing [this], the crowds were amazed at his teaching.

Reading 3   Matthew 22:34–40

διδάσκαλε	voc sg masc, διδάσκαλος
ἀγαπήσεις	2ᵈ sg fut act ind, ἀγαπάω
ὅλῃ	dat sg fem, ὅλος

34. And the Pharisees, hearing that he silenced the Sadducees, were gathered to the same [place]. 35. And one from them, a lawyer, asked, testing him, 36. "Teacher, which is the great commandment in the law?"

37. And he said to him, "You shall love the Lord your God with your whole heart and with your whole soul and with your whole mind; 38. this is the great and first commandment. 39. And a second [is] similar to it, You shall love your neighbor as yourself. 40. In these two commandments all the law and the prophets are hanging."

Reading 4   Matthew 22:41–46

συνηγμένων	gen pl masc perf mid/pass part, συνάγω
θῶ	1ˢᵗ sg aor act subj, τίθημι
ἐπερωτῆσαι	aor act inf, ἐπερωτάω

41. And after the Pharisees were gathered, Jesus asked them, 42. saying, "What does it seem to you concerning the Christ? Whose son is he?" They said to him, "Of David."

43. He said to them, "Then how did David, in the Spirit, call him Lord, saying,

44. '[The] Lord said to my Lord, "Sit at my right, until I place your enemies under your feet" '?

45. Therefore if David calls him Lord, how is he his son?" 46. And no one was able to answer a word to him, nor [did] anyone dare from that day to question him any longer.

Reading 5   Matthew 23:1–7

εἴπωσιν	3d pl aor act subj, λέγω
φιλοῦσιν	3d pl pres act ind, φιλέω
καλεῖσθαι	pres mid/pass inf, καλέω

1. Then Jesus spoke to the crowds and to his disciples 2. saying, "The scribes and Pharisees sat on the seat of Moses. 3. Therefore all things, whatever they say to you, do and keep, but do not do according to their works; for they speak and do not do. 4. And they bind heavy burdens and they place [them] on the shoulders of people, but they with their finger are not willing to move them.

5. And they do all their works in order to be seen by people; for they widen their phylacteries and make long the tassels of their garments. 6. And they love the place of honor in the banquets and the best seats in the synagogues, 7. and the greetings in the marketplaces and to be called by people, 'Rabbi.'"

Reading 6   Matthew 23:8–13

κληθῆτε	2d pl aor pass subj, καλέω
καλέσητε	2d pl aor act subj, καλέω
ἀφίετε	2d pl pres act ind, ἀφίημι

8. "But you, do not be called, 'Rabbi,' for One is your Teacher, and all of you are brothers. 9. And do not call [anyone] your father on the earth, for One is your heavenly Father. 10. And do not be called teachers, because your Teacher is One, the Christ. 11. But the greatest of you will be your servant. 12. And whoever will exalt himself will be humbled, and whoever will humble himself will be exalted.

13. And woe to you, scribes and Pharisees, hypocrites, because you shut the kingdom of heaven before people; for you [yourselves] do not go in, nor do you allow to enter the ones who are entering."

Week Nine

Reading 1   John 6:60–65

εἰδὼς	nom sg masc perf act part, οἶδα
εἴρηκα	1st sg perf act ind, λέγω
δεδομένον	nom sg neut perf mid/pass part, δίδωμι

60. Therefore, many from his disciples, after hearing, said, "This word is hard; who is able to hear it?"

61. But Jesus, knowing in himself that his disciples were grumbling about this, said to them, "Does this offend you? 62. Thus [what] if you should see the Son of Man ascending [to] where he was before? 63. The Spirit is the one who gives life, the flesh benefits nothing; the words that I have spoken to you are spirit and they are life. 64. But there are some of you who do not believe." For Jesus knew from the beginning who were the ones who would not believe and who was the one who would betray him. 65. And he said, "On account of this I have told you that no one is able to come to me unless it has been given to him from the Father."

Reading 2   John 6:66–71

περιεπάτουν	3d pl impf act ind, περιπατέω
ἀπελευσόμεθα	1st pl fut mid ind, ἀπέρχομαι
ἔμελλεν	3d sg impf act ind, μέλλω

66. From this [time] many from his disciples went away to the back and they were no longer walking with him.

67. Therefore Jesus said to the Twelve, "You don't also wish to go away, do you?"

68. Simon Peter answered him, "Lord, to whom will we go? You have the words of eternal life, 69. and we have believed and we have known that you are the Holy One of God."

70. Jesus answered them, "Did I not choose you, the Twelve, yet one from you is a devil?" 71. Now he was speaking [about] Judas [the son] of Simon Iscariot; for this one was intending to betray him, being one from the Twelve.

Reading 3   John 7:1–7

ἤθελεν	3d sg impf act ind, θέλω
εἶπον	3d pl aor act ind, λέγω
μισεῖν	pres act inf, μισέω

1. And after these things, Jesus was walking in Galilee; for he was not willing to walk in Judea, because the Jews were seeking him to kill. 2. But the festival of the Jews, the Feast of Tabernacles, was near. 3. Therefore his brothers said to him, "Depart from here and go away into Judea, so that also your disciples will see your works that you do. 4. For no one does anything in secret yet seeks himself to be in public view. If you do these things reveal yourself to the world." 5. For his brothers were not believing in him.

6. Thus Jesus said to them, "My time is not yet present, but your time always is ready. 7. The world is not able to hate you, but it hates me, because I bear witness concerning it, that its works are evil.

Reading 4   John 7:8–13

ἀνάβητε	2ᵈ pl aor act impt, ἀναβαίνω
εἰπών	nom sg masc aor act part, λέγω
πλανᾷ	3ᵈ sg pres act ind, πλανάω

8. "[As for] you, go up to the festival; I am not going up to this festival, because my time has not yet been fulfilled." 9. And after saying these things, he remained in Galilee.

10. But when his brothers went up to the festival, then also he went up, not openly, but as in secret. 11. So the Jews were seeking him at the festival and they were saying, "Where is that [man]?"

12. And there was much whispering concerning him among the crowds; some were saying, "He is [a] good [man]," but others were saying, "No, rather he deceives the crowd." 13. No one however was speaking openly about him on account of the fear of the Jews.

Reading 5   John 7:14–19

μεμαθηκώς	nom sg masc perf act part, μανθάνω
ζητεῖ	3ᵈ sg pres act ind, ζητέω
δέδωκεν	3ᵈ sg perf act ind, δίδωμι

14. But now the feast being in the middle, Jesus went up to the temple and was teaching.

15. Therefore the Jews were marveling, saying, "How does this [man] know the letters since he has not learned?"

16. So Jesus answered them and said, "My teaching is not mine, but of the One who sent me. 17. If anyone wishes to do his will, he will know about the teaching whether it is from God or I speak from myself. 18. The one who speaks from himself seeks his own glory; but the one who seeks the glory of the One who sent him, this [man] is true and there is no unrighteousness in him. 19. Has not Moses given the law to you? Still none of you does the law. Why do you seek to kill me?"

Reading 6   John 7:20–24

λυθῇ	3ᵈ sg aor pass subj, λύω
ἐποίησα	1ˢᵗ sg aor act ind, ποιέω
δικαίαν	acc sg fem, δίκαιος

20. The crowd answered, "You have a demon; who seeks to kill you?"

21. Jesus answered and said to them, "I did one work and you all marvel. 22. On account of this Moses has given circumcision to you—not that it is from Moses but from the fathers—and you circumcise a person on the Sabbath. 23. If a man receives circumcision on a Sabbath, so that the law of Moses might not be broken, [why] are you angry with me because I made a whole man healthy on [a] Sabbath? 24. Do not judge according to outward appearance, but judge the just judgment."

Week Ten

Reading 1   John 8:12–16

ἐλάλησεν	3ᵈ sg aor act ind, λαλέω
περιπατήσῃ	3ᵈ sg aor act subj, περιπατέω
ἀληθινή	nom sg fem, ἀληθινός

12. Then again Jesus spoke to them, saying, "I am the light of the world; the one who follows me will not walk in the darkness, but will have the light of life."

13. So the Pharisees said to him, "You witness concerning yourself; your witness is not true."

14. Jesus answered and said to them, "Even if I witness concerning myself, my witness is true, because I know from where I came and where I go; but you do not know from where I come or where I go. 15. You judge according to the flesh, I do not judge anyone. 16. But even if I judge, my judgment is true, because I am not alone, but I and the Father who sent me [judge]."

Reading 2   John 8:17–21

γέγραπται	3ᵈ sg perf mid/pass ind, γράφω
ζητήσετε	2ᵈ pl fut act ind, ζητέω
ἀποθανεῖσθε	2ᵈ pl fut mid ind, ἀποθνῄσκω

17. "And even in your law it has been written that the witness of two people is true. 18. I am the one who witnesses concerning myself and the Father who sent me witnesses concerning me."

19. Therefore they were saying to him, "Where is your father?" Jesus answered, "You know neither me nor my Father; if you knew, also you would know my Father."[12] 20. He spoke these words in the treasury, while teaching

---

[12]The ἄν (coupled with the εἰ at the beginning of the sentence) signifies that this is a second-class condition (the contrary-to-fact condition). In a second-class condition, the protasis is assumed to be untrue—*if you knew me* (in fact, they do not know him) (*BBG*, 330; Wallace, 694–96).

in the temple; and no one arrested him, because his hour had not yet come.

21. Thus again he said to them, "I am going away and you will seek me, and you will die in your sin; where I am going you are not able to come."

Reading 3   John 8:22–27

ἀποκτενεῖ	3ᵈ sg fut act ind, ἀποκτείνω
ἁμαρτίαις	dat pl fem, ἁμαρτία
ἔγνωσαν	3ᵈ pl aor act ind, γινώσκω

22. So the Jews were saying, "He won't kill himself, will he, because he says, 'Where I am going, you are not able to come'?"

23. And he was saying to them, "You are of the things below, I am of the things above; you are from this world, I am not from this world.

24. Therefore I said to you that you will die in your sins; for if you do not believe that I am, you will die in your sins."

25. Thus they were saying to him, "Who are you?" Jesus said to them, "How is it that I even speak to you at all? 26. I have many things to say and to judge about you; but the One who sent me is true, and I, what I heard from him, I speak these things in the world."

27. They did not know that he was speaking [about] the Father to them.

Reading 4   John 8:28–33

ἐμαυτοῦ	gen sg masc, ἐμαυτοῦ
ἀφῆκέν	3ᵈ sg aor act ind, ἀφίημι
ἐσμεν	1ˢᵗ pl pres act ind, εἰμί

28. Then Jesus said, "When you lift up the Son of Man, then you will know that I am, and [that] I do nothing from myself, but as the Father taught me, these things I speak. 29. And the One who sent me is with me; he did not leave me alone, because I always do the things pleasing to him." 30. As he said these things, many believed in him.

31. Thus Jesus was saying to the Jews who had believed in him, "If you remain in my word, you are truly my disciples, 32. and you will know the truth, and the truth will free you."

33. They answered to him, "We are the seed of Abraham and we have served no one ever; how do you say, 'You will be free'?"

Reading 5   John 8:34–40

ποιῶν	nom sg masc pres act part, ποιέω
ἑώρακα	1ˢᵗ sg perf act ind, ὁράω
τέκνα	nom pl neut, τέκνον

34. Jesus answered to them, "Truly, truly, I say to you that everyone who is doing sin is a slave of sin. 35. And the slave does not remain in the house forever,[13] the son remains forever. 36. Therefore if the Son frees you, you will be really free. 37. I know that you are the offspring of Abraham; but you seek to kill me, because my word does not make progress among you. 38. What things I have seen beside the Father, I speak; therefore, also what things you heard from [your] father you do."

39. They answered and said to him, "Our father is Abraham." Jesus said to them, "If you were children of Abraham, you would do the works of Abraham. 40. But now you seek to kill me, a man who has spoken the truth to you, which I heard from God; this Abraham did not do."

Reading 6   John 8:41–45

γεγεννήμεθα	1ˢᵗ pl perf mid/pass ind, γεννάω
ἐλήλυθα	1ˢᵗ sg perf act ind, ἔρχομαι
λαλῇ	3ᵈ sg pres act subj, λαλέω

41. "You do the works of your father." They said to him, "We have not been born of fornication; we have one Father, God."

42. Jesus said to them, "If God were your father, you would love me, for I come out from God and have arrived; for not from myself have I come, but that One sent me. 43. Why do you not understand my speech? Because you are not able to hear my word. 44. You are from [your] father, the devil and you wish to do the desires of your father. That one was a murderer from the beginning and he was not standing in the truth, because truth is not in him. Whenever he speaks the lie, he speaks from his own things, because he is a liar and the father of it. 45. But because I speak the truth, you do not believe me."

---

[13]See the note at Reading 5 of Week Four for this expression.

Week Eleven

Reading 1	Mark 13:3–8
καθημένου	gen sg masc pres mid/pass part, κάθημαι
μέλλη	3ᵈ sg pres act subj, μέλλω
ἔσονται	3ᵈ pl fut mid ind, εἰμί

3. And as he sat on the Mountain of Olives opposite the temple Peter and James and John and Andrew were questioning him privately, 4. "Say to us when will these things be, and what the sign [will be] when all these things are about to be completed."

5. And Jesus began to say to them, "Watch lest anyone deceive you; 6. many will come in my name, saying 'I am,' and they will deceive many. 7. But whenever you hear [of] wars and reports of wars, do not be frightened; it is necessary to happen, but the end [is] not yet. 8. For a nation will rise against a nation and a kingdom against a kingdom, there will be earthquakes in places, there will be famines; these things [are] the beginning of birth pains."

Reading 2	Mark 13:9–13
συναγωγὰς	acc pl fem, συναγωγή
σταθήσεσθε	2ᵈ pl fut pass ind, ἵστημι
δοθῇ	3ᵈ sg aor pass subj, δίδωμι

9. "But as for you, watch yourselves; they will hand you over to the councils and you will be beaten in synagogues and you will stand before governors and kings on account of me, for a testimony to them. 10. And to all the nations first it is necessary [for] the gospel to be proclaimed. 11. And when they lead you, delivering [you], do not worry beforehand [about] what you will say, but whatever is given to you in that hour, speak this, for you are not the ones who speak but the Holy Spirit.

12. And brother will betray brother to death and a father [will betray] a child, and children will rise in rebellion against parents and will kill them; 13. and you will be hated by all on account of my name. But the one who endures to the end, this one will be saved."

Reading 3	Mark 13:14–19
ἆραι	aor act inf, αἴρω
ἐκεῖναι	nom pl fem, ἐκεῖνος
γένηται	3ᵈ sg aor mid subj, γίνομαι

14. "But whenever you see the abomination of desolation standing where it should not, let the one reading understand, then let those in Judea flee into the mountains, 15. and let the one on the housetop not descend, nor let him enter to take anything from his house, 16. and let the one in the field not return back to take his garment. 17. And woe to those having [babies] in the womb and to those who are nursing in those days. 18. But pray that it might not be during winter; 19. for those days will be suffering such as has not happened of this kind from the beginning of creation, which God created, until now and will never happen."

Reading 4	Mark 13:20–25
ἐσώθη	3ᵈ sg aor pass ind, σώζω
ἐξελέξατο	3ᵈ sg aor mid ind, ἐκλέγομαι
ἐγερθήσονται	3ᵈ pl fut pass ind, ἐγείρω

20. "And if the Lord did not shorten the days, not any flesh would be saved. But on account of the elect, whom he chose, he shortened the days. 21. And then, if anyone says to you, 'See, here [is] the Christ,' 'See there,' do not believe; 22. for false Christs and false prophets will be raised up and they will give signs and portents in order to mislead, if possible, the elect. 23. But as for you, watch; I have told you all beforehand.

24. But in those days after that affliction, the sun will be darkened and the moon will not give its light,

25. and the stars will be falling from heaven and the powers, the ones in heaven, will be shaken."

Reading 5	Mark 13:26–31
ὄψονται	3ᵈ pl fut mid ind, ὁράω
μάθετε	2ᵈ pl aor act impt, μανθάνω
θύραις	dat pl fem, θύρα

26. "And then they will see the Son of Man coming in [the] clouds with much power and glory. 27. And then he will send the angels and he will gather together his elect from the four winds, from the extreme end of [the] earth to the extreme end of heaven.

28. But learn the parable from the fig tree; when already its branch becomes tender and puts forth leaves, you know that summer is near. 29. Thus also you, when you see these things happening, you know that it is near, at [the] doors. 30. Truly, I say to you that this generation will not at all pass away until all these things happen. 31. The heaven and the earth will pass away, but my words will not at all pass away."

Reading 6   Mark 13:32–37

ἀφείς	nom sg masc aor act part, ἀφίημι
δούς	nom sg masc aor act part, δίδωμι
εὕρῃ	3ᵈ sg aor act subj, εὑρίσκω

32. "But concerning that day or hour no one knows, neither the angels in heaven nor the Son, [no one] except the Father. 33. Watch, be awake; for you do not know when the appointed time is. 34. [It is] like an absent man leaving his house and giving authority to his servants, to each his work, and he gave orders to the doorkeeper that he should be alert.

35. Therefore be alert, for you do not know when the lord of the house is coming whether in the evening or at midnight or at cock's crow or early in the morning, 36. lest coming unexpectedly he might find you sleeping. 37. And what I say to you, I say to all, be alert!"

Week Twelve

Reading 1   John 5:1–7

ἦν	3ᵈ sg impf act ind, εἰμί
γνούς	nom sg masc aor act part, γινώσκω
βάλῃ	3ᵈ sg aor act subj, βάλλω

1. After these things there was a feast of the Jews, and Jesus went up to Jerusalem. 2. And there was in Jerusalem, at the sheep gate, a pool that is called in Hebrew "Bethzatha," having five porches. 3. Among these [porches] a large number of those who were sick, blind, lame, [or] withered were reclining.[14] 5. And there was a certain man in that place who had [been] in his illness thirty-eight years; 6. Jesus, seeing this man lying, and knowing that he had [been sick] already for a long time, said to him, "Do you wish to become healthy?"

7. The one who was sick answered him, "Lord, I do not have a man so that when the water is stirred he might put me into the pool; but in which [time] I come, another before me descends."

Reading 2   John 5:8–13

ἆρον	2ᵈ sg aor act impt, αἴρω
τεθεραπευμένῳ	dat sg masc perf mid/pass part, θεραπεύω
ἰαθείς	nom sg masc aor pass part, ἰάομαι

8. Jesus said to him, "Rise, take up your mattress and walk." 9. And immediately the man became healthy, and he took up his mattress and was walking. But it was a Sabbath on that day. 10. Then the Jews were saying to the one who had been healed, "It is a Sabbath, and it is not lawful for you to take up your mattress."

11. But he answered them, "The one who made me healthy, that one said to me, 'Take up your mattress and walk.'"

12. They asked him, "Who is the man who said to you, 'Take up and walk'?"

13. But the one who had been healed did not know who he was, for Jesus withdrew [from] a crowd being in the place.

Reading 3   John 5:14–19

ἁμάρτανε	2ᵈ sg pres act impt, ἁμαρτάνω
ἀπεκρίνατο	3ᵈ sg aor mid ind, ἀποκρίνομαι
ἔλυεν	3ᵈ sg impf act ind, λύω

14. After these things, Jesus found him in the temple and said to him, "See, you have become healthy; sin no longer, lest something worse happen to you." 15. The man went away and reported to the Jews that Jesus was the one who made him healthy.

16. And on account of this the Jews were pursuing Jesus, because he was doing these things on a Sabbath. 17. But Jesus answered them, "My Father until now works, and I work." 18. Therefore on account of this, more [than ever] the Jews were seeking to kill him, because not only was he breaking the Sabbath but also he was calling his own Father God, making himself equal to God.

19. Therefore Jesus answered and was saying to them, "Truly, truly, I say to you, the Son is not able to do nothing from himself except what he sees the Father doing; for whatever things that one does, these things also the Son, likewise, does."

Reading 4   John 5:20–26

δείξει	3ᵈ sg fut act ind, δείκνυμι
τιμῶσι	3ᵈ pl pres act subj, τιμάω
τιμᾷ	3ᵈ sg pres act ind, τιμάω

20. "For the Father loves the Son and shows to him all things that he does, and greater works than these will he show to him, so that you might be amazed. 21. For as the Father raises the dead and gives life, so also the Son gives

[14]Verse 4 is omitted in the oldest and best manuscripts.

life [to] whom he wishes. 22. For the Father does not judge anyone, but he has given all judgment to the Son, 23. so that all might honor the Son as they honor the Father. The one who does not honor the Son does not honor the Father who sent him.

24. Truly, truly, I say to you that the one hearing my word and believing the One who sent me has life eternal and does not come into judgment, but has passed over out of death into life. 25. Truly, truly, I say to you that an hour is coming and now is when the dead will hear the voice of the Son of God and the ones who hear will live. 26. For as the Father has life in himself, so also he gave to the Son to have life in himself."

Reading 5	**John 5:27–32**
μνημείοις	dat pl neut, μνημεῖον
πράξαντες	nom pl masc aor act part, πράσσω
πέμψαντός	gen sg masc aor act part, πέμπω

27. "And he gave authority to him to make judgment, because he is the Son of Man.

28. Do not marvel [at] this, because an hour is coming in which all those in the tombs will hear his voice 29. and they will come out, the ones who did the good things into a resurrection of life, but those who did the bad things into a resurrection of judgment. 30. I am not able to do any-

thing from myself; as I hear, I judge, and my judgment is just, because I do not seek my will but the will of the One who sent me.

31. If I testify concerning myself, my witness is not true; 32. another is the One who witnesses concerning me, and I know that the testimony is true which he testifies concerning me."

Reading 6	**John 5:33–38**
σωθῆτε	2d pl aor pass subj, σῴζω
ἠθελήσατε	2d pl aor act ind, θέλω
μένοντα	acc sg masc pres act part, μένω

33. "You have sent to John and he has testified to the truth; 34. but I do not receive testimony from people, but these things I say so that you might be saved. 35. That [man] was the lamp that burns and shines, and you wished to exult for an hour in his light.

36. But I have the witness greater than [the witness of] John; for the works that the Father has given to me that I might complete them, the works themselves which I do testify about me that the Father has sent me; 37. and the Father who sent me, that One has witnessed about me. Never have you heard his voice nor have you seen his form, 38. and you do not have his word remaining in you, because whom that One sent, you do not believe this one."

9 780310 236603